TO

_____

FROM

_____

Let's Be an INSPIRATION to the next GENERATION

INSPIRE ONE

How to become an INSPIRATION to this Next GENERATION

JONATHAN OSORIO

DEDICATED TO YOU

Before you were born, God placed an incredible potential in you. It is not an accident that you are holding this book. God longs for you to see how much He loves you, has gifted you with, to make a difference with your family, community, and the World.

I want to thank you for taking the time to read this book. For desiring to learn more on how to be an Inspiration to the Next Generation. I believe there is something in this book that can equip, inspire, and empower you to make a difference in your home, church, community, and the World.

I would like to thank my best friend, my Lord and Savior: Jesus Christ. I thank Him for the Inspiration that He has been in my life, and for inspiring me to write this book. To my wife, Vanessa Osorio, for believing in me since the first day, and her unconditional and relentless love towards me. To my son Joziah and Izaiah for the joy, patience, and laughter they bring to my life. Lastly, I want to dedicate this book to my family and friends for their support, love, and sacrifice. Live to Inspire others.

CONTENTS

Foreword 9

Part 1: POTENTIAL 13

Chapter 1: Underestimated 15
Chapter 2: Am I not Good Enough? 20
Chapter 3: You Are Wanted 26
Chapter 4: Everyone Has a Story but No One Has Your Story 32
Chapter 5: Something Huge Is Inside of You. 37

Part 2: PERSPECTIVE 48

Chapter 6: Picture Perspective 49
Chapter 7: From Surrounded To Grounded 52
Chapter 8: Prescribed Perspective 56
Chapter 9: You Got This! 61
Chapter 10: Your Connections influence Your Direction 66
Chapter 11: A Crazy Perspective 71

Part 3: POSITION 77

Chapter 12: Cleaning Toilets 78
Chapter 13: Where Have You Been Positioned? 84
Chapter 14: Positioned to Conquer 92
Chapter 15: Want to be Great? 99
Chapter 16: Patient with the Process 107

FOREWORD

First off, thank you for picking up this book, and taking the time out of your busy day to read and learn how you can be an inspiration to this next generation. There must be a desire in you to leave an impact, a legacy or you might just want to learn how to inspire others. Think about this, what is more fulfilling than someone coming up to you years later and telling you: "Thank you, because of you my life was impacted forever."

In this book, we are going to look at it from a Biblical perspective. For the past two years, I have studied the Gospels: Matthew, Mark, Luke, and John. I have seen how Jesus was able to invite and inspire twelve young lives to come alongside Him. These twelve disciples leave everything from their families, friends, and houses, businesses to learn from Jesus and through it, change the world.

Whether you are a young person who just got this book and does not have a clue who Jesus is, or you have grown up in the church, I pray this book becomes an inspiration to your life. I hope it allows you to see how crazy our Heavenly Father is about you, and the gifts and talents that He has instilled inside of you. You are the only you, that will ever exist. You are unique, gifted, chosen, and loved. Think about this for a moment, there will never be another you. Yes, you because everyone else is already taken! I pray something awakens in your life and you start to see your life, from a heavenly perspective and position yourself for God to use you.

Now, if you are a youth leader, thank you for your dedication and commitment to this generation. We need you! We could not do this without your help. This book was created to help you be aware of the amazing potential found in the youth you are leading. Whether you are leading three or one hundred, numbers are nothing when it comes to God using us. So, stop counting, and start with what God has placed in front of you. Look at Gideon who was going to war. It was not until God cut his numbers to only 300 that resulted in him winning the war. He then realized this was only accomplished through God's power and spirit. I pray you can use this book to help the youth in your class, church, community to see their God-gifted potential, share with them a perspective and position them. And remember this:

"No one is ever too young, too small, too little, for God to use"

MY PROMISE

Through God's help, I commit the next 16 weeks of my life to read one chapter a week with a friend to discover how to INSPIRE the NEXT GENERATION.

_____
YOUR NAME

_____
FRIEND'S NAME

Life was meant to be lived and experienced together.

PART 1: POTENTIAL

Potential is what awakens a dream, inspires a soul, and renews a heart. Potential is what is placed within every human heart. It is a seed that has its home in each life.

Potential is granted to every human life that has ever had the opportunity to set foot on planet earth. That would include you reading this book. Because last time I checked, you were placed in this world because you have a purpose that is grounded in the potential to do great and mighty things.

You might not feel it right now, you might not see it right now, you might not even think it right now, but if you begin to water and fertilize that seed of potential inside you, I'm telling you, it will burst from the ground.

CHAPTER 1

UNDERESTIMATED

"The first step to resolve a problem is to recognize there is one"

As a youth pastor, I enjoy working with the next generation. Listening to their dreams, aspirations, and wanting to make a difference in our world today. As I connect with many of these youth and young adults. I have heard many experiences where youth or young adults felt there was no space or place for them in the church. It reminded me of my own experience. I remember from an early age, I and many other young lives were underestimated, look down, not given the time to listen or hear what we envisioned church to be. Now many of those church friends have just walked away from the church.

We need to see that there is a something happening within our churches, communities, and families that revolves around not allowing or giving our young people the space to listen and learn. Let me begin with the reason why I felt Inspired to write this book.

It kills me and breaks my heart, to see how church leaders underestimate the potential of our youth. I have seen countless young lives, including my own, who have been affected by it. I believe it's time that we as youth leaders begin to see the potential that this generation has and to speak into their lives by helping them realize the full God gifted potential, so they can leave a mark and an impact in the world today.

Something that has helped me learn about how to connect with the youth or young adults is inviting them out to eat. Just taking them out and spending that one-on-one time with them. In these conversations I have seen how it unlocks many of their struggles, dreams and aspirations that are just waiting to come out. I have noticed throughout my lunch and dinner visitations with the youth or young adults that they are desperate to give their talents to God, but they are constantly shut down by the leadership, and they begin to question what their purpose really is, whether it is within the church or society. To a certain extent, I do not blame them because looking back on my life; there were many times that I kept asking myself the same question. What is my purpose in life? Where am I going? Why am I here? Who am I? Maybe you have asked the same questions in this season of your life.

As a Pastor I encountered this story as I was moving to Houston, Texas. I remember when my wife and I had just driven 34 long hours from Los Angeles, California to Houston, Texas. We had been married for only 15 days. My brother and my son Wes (which for the record is our dog) were with us. After we arrived in Houston, one day, I went to the bank to open an account with my wife. We were called and asked to sit down and started to open our account. The bank employee began to ask us how long we had been living in Houston. This was a typical question to ask to break the ice. We said like 2 or 3 days so then he asked us where we had come from? I had my fitted LA Dodger hat on because you know I was representing my city and I said with my LA accent "I'm from L.A." (Los Angeles), and the next question he asked was what brings you to Houston, Texas? I said, "A Calling". His face looked so confused and said "Calling?" "Yea" I responded. he was like "For what?" "To be a pastor at a church in Houston," I said. his face dropped, and the next three words that he said were: "You're a Pastor?" I knew what was going on his head. This youngster is a Pastor. Isn't he too young to be a Pastor? Maybe the way I was dressed did not reflect that I was a pastor being that I was rocking my LA fitted hat with my shorts and a white tee cause if you've ever been to Houston around August two words that you need to know and remember is it is CRAZY HOT IN AUGUST!

Coming back to the encounter, let's be real, when you think of a Pastor, you think of someone who usually is much older.

It happens to me every day, with people from church. I have noticed how people outside the church are a little more gracious. But people from church say things like…how is this young preacher with little experience in life going to teach me? Why is he not wearing a suit? Why the colored socks (by the way, I love colored socks)? The list can go on.

Church culture has developed the attitude that to be a Pastor; you must be a certain age or look a certain way or talk in a certain way.

I can imagine you to have felt the same way of being looked down upon, without seeing the potential that you have. It is time you unlock the God-gifted potential that he has placed within you. As a youth or young adult, it's time we see the God gifted Potential that we have to make a difference. It is time to unlock the dreams and visions that are burning inside and start living them every day. It is time you recognize that you are loved beyond your physical looks, beyond your imperfections, beyond your past, failures, or mistakes, and loved beyond anything you can ever accomplish. You are just loved.

It is time for youth or young adults to speak words of life into their youth's lives and make them aware of what God can do through a young life and the impact they can have on their generation. It is time that you as a youth or young adult recognize that you might not know it all, you might be weak, but let me just tell you that God delights in your weakness and works best with weakness. You don't believe me? Check out His word in 2 Corinthians 12:9-10 (MSG) it says:

> "My Grace is enough; it is all you need. My strength comes into its own in your weakness… I just let Christ take over! And so, the weaker I get, the stronger I become."

Here is another one:

> "Their weakness was turned to strength. They became strong in battle and put whole armies to flight." (Hebrews 11:34 NLT)

And let me give you one more:

"God chose the weak things of this world to tame the wise."
(1 Corinthians 1:27)

I want you to realize and recognize the God-given POTENTIAL he has placed inside you and a PERSPECTIVE to see beyond our human limitations and no matter the place you are and how God has POSITIONED you to achieve greater things.

"Don't let anyone look down on you but set an example to all the believers in the way you speak, in the way you live, in your love, your faith, and purity." -1 Timothy 4:12 (NLT)

CHAPTER 2

AM I NOT GOOD ENOUGH?

"Don't underestimate me. I know more than I say, think more than I speak, and notice more than you realize."

This is one question that I noticed was discussed a lot when I asked several millennial and generation Z, and it unlocked a depth of emotions. Before I unlock many of these stories and share them with you, I would love you to listen to their hearts

The one question I asked them all was "How have you been looked down upon at church, by family or in your community? And why? Here is what they shared.

College Student:

The story I'm about to share with you is a story of a youth from our Sabbath School class. Today as I talked with this youth, I learned a lot about what goes on in his life. He just began his first year in college. Out of the week, he spent 6 days at work from 6am and worked until 11 am faithfully stocking the shelves at Joann's. He did not grow up with a father figure at home, he is from immigrant parents, but considering the odds, he is a very hard worker. When you look into his eyes, you can see that he has been through a lot in his 18 years of life. He has been looked down upon by his teachers in high school. They have belittled him by saying things such as: "You are going to end up in jail" or "You are not good for anything." Some even went to the extent of yelling at him. What surprised him the most was that he thought the principal would have at least treated him with respect and dignity, but instead, he was treated with anger and disrespect.

Theology Student:

Regarding his church experience, "I feel that most of the churches I have attended have been more worried about keeping the traditions and doctrine than actually caring about the spiritual well-being of the church. We are more worried about the church (what's in between the walls) then who isn't there. We need to be a church that is reaching out, looking to bring back those who are gone and reaching out to people who have never given their lives to Christ. We need to progress as a church, and you would see more people in our church." I felt like I could not use my talents because I was too progressive. My pastor walked off the platform when I was leading worship because it was not hymns. This is me with an acoustic guitar, no drums or electric guitar. This was my experience of church.

High Schooler:

Regarding my high school experience. "Because I don't like to do what they do, they started to push me away and I lost my friends because I just didn't want to do it. I noticed they looked down on me because every time I would sit with them, they would get up and leave."

Young Leader:

My Experience of pop culture and church. "Well, I have been looked down upon in many ways, especially for being a Christian. I have been physically assaulted and insulted. This world has changed dramatically. Being a young Christian is one of the most challenging things that I have faced. When you say "I am a Christian" to the world, it is like you are admitting in some way a lack of understanding and seems like you cannot think for yourself, or it is like saying that I am a religious bigot just because I believe in Jesus. This is due to the misconception people have about Jesus Christ. When talking about being looked down on in the church, well it is a touchy subject, and it's something that we do not want to admit, but it does exist. I am the type of young person, like many, that loves Christ and loves working for Him. Sometimes people at church would get uncomfortable seeing that passion for Christ's work. As a result, they would say negative comments to put me down or discourage me by talking behind my back thinking I was weird."

Ex-Youth Leader:

My Experience in Church. "Well, when we were working with the youth group at church sometimes to do an afternoon program, vespers, or holiday program, the (Church Leadership) always had such a high expectation from us. I guess because we were young, they always expected us to have a program that would make a big impact on current events. They would always ask what ideas we had to bring youth into the church, and how to make our programs more interesting. There was a huge amount of pressure to perform. We would work hard and try to have a balance of presenting something spiritual where everyone can take something with them. I remember this one time we worked hard on a skit. The skit was going to be a narrative about a son. We had people of all ages helping. The skit was about a girl fighting with her issues from boyfriend problems to being bullied, resorting to drugs, being sexually molested until she ran to Jesus. She notices the spiritual battle, but Jesus wins it for her. Well, after the play, we got spoken to. We were told we were too young to understand that these kinds of programs are not church related. To them, what we did was unacceptable, and we were told we had to be supervised. It was wrong to show those issues because our youth were going to get crazy ideas."

Another idea was when we formed a vespers group, and the youth met every Friday, and our Pastor had the sermon for us. We did a Revelation Seminar, which was great. Then we were told by the elders that our group did not count as a vespers group, and it was not going to be taken into consideration to participate with other vespers group at the church because to them, we were not a serious group. It is sad because we were actually studying the Bible, and we even had a Daniel seminar after the Revelation, but they ignored our request.

Young Pastor:

    My Experience as a Pastor. "I was looked down on as a Pastor for not having enough Experience."

Born in the Church:

    My Experience in Church. "Well personally, I get a lot of stares for my beard, shaved head, tattoos, and piercings and so on. I came to notice that Hispanic parents have a picture in their heads of what we as Christians should look like, and anything that wavers from that is seen as bad or disobedient. I get looked down on for how I look, regardless of where my mind is at or what my spiritual walk with God is.

    What is this youth or young adult going to teach me? What experience has this youth pastor lived that will influence or impact my life? What is this professional fresh out of college going to show me? How many years have you lived? You still have a lot to live. You are too young. You need to gain more experience. You will one day get there. You have a lot of growing and maturing to do first."

    All these experiences resonate in the minds and hearts of many youth and young adults today. Without ever relating to our understand them and listening to them.

I can imagine you might have had an experience where you have been looked down, underestimated at school, work, church, community, or family. Many of you have been affected and hurt. In talking to many of them, they have either walked away from their home, church or family and do not know where they can have a safe place to grow in their faith journey.

CHAPTER 3

YOU ARE WANTED

"If our Youth rise and act, they have the strength and dynamism to generate a huge transformation in society."

I love playing sports, but basketball is my favorite sport. One day, as I was playing basketball at L.A. Fitness. As I was playing basketball on a Sunday morning, I introduced myself to one of our teammates who was our point guard at the end of one of the games. The way he played basketball caught my attention. He reminded me of the basketball players back in Los Angeles. He was short, but he could hold his ground, had handles, could dribble, had a nice jump shot, and was a nice passer. I was curious to know where he was from. I went straight up to him after the basketball game and asked him where he was from. He told me he was from Los Angeles, California.

In talking to him he started to share his story with me. He was from Los Angeles, California and had come to Houston about 10-12 years ago. I asked him "why?" he said because things were looking rough in Los Angeles. Many of his friends were getting shot at and killed as a result of gang violence. I asked him if he was ever a gang member. He said he was never one, but all his friends and family members were part of a gang. I was like, you being able to experience it firsthand, what is it that moved your friends and family members to join a gang? He said many of my friends and family members never grew up with a father figure at home. Many of them had a house to go to and sleep in, but no home where they were loved, cared, and belonged. They were looking for a community they could be a part of a brotherhood.

    I asked how old were you when your friends decided to join a gang. He said he remembers clearly that many of the gang members would recruit as early as a middle schooler around the ages of 13, 14, and 15 years old. I was shocked to hear this from a person that had lived it firsthand and had seen the violence and death of many of his homies and friends. He later goes on to tell me that he had seen enough because, in that same week, three of his friends were killed in a drive-by shooting. With little to nothing in his bank account, he said he left Los Angeles and headed to Houston where all he had was an aunt. Now as he reflects back 12 years later, he realized that was one of the best decisions he made for himself and his wife, and now he has a beautiful family with two daughters.

    When we continued playing basketball, I could not play with the same intensity. The reasons being is that it hit me hard what he had shared with me, and I started to imagine how many young teenagers, at this moment, in different middle schools, are being recruited to be part of a gang because they are looking for a place where they can be loved, cared for, and belong. A community where they can exist, have a purpose, identity, or reason for living. It broke my heart because even the gangs are doing more recruitment than our churches are. You might be asking how this is possible. For many years, I kept hearing from the front of the pulpit that the youth are the church of tomorrow. They are our future when just a couple blocks away, they are being told that there is a place for them right there, right then, and right now. They want a community that they can be a part of, where they can feel safe, be loved, cared for and belong.

Another story that I remember was when I was about 17 years old. It was my senior year. The year was 2006. Class of 06. We used to put up three fingers on each side representing and throwing up the number six as an indication of our year and shouting the words "06". Many Seniors do something to let the whole student body know who the Seniors are, and to remind them what year they are graduating. I know if you finished high school, then you did something similar to it or even if you are reading this and still in high school, I'm just letting you know you are going to do something along these lines. Just for the record throwing up the three fingers on each hand and crossing them was not gang-related, even though if you looked at some pictures, it can easily be depicted as one. We were just having fun and making sure all the freshman, sophomore, and juniors knew who the seniors were, and what year it was. I know looking back, it was pretty foolish, but when you are Senior, you do not think so.

Coming back to the story, I was at the mall with my mom escorting her and taking care of her. Now you've got to get a little background to who my mom is. She is from a small country called El

Salvador. She is a short little woman full of love for everyone, but at the same time, protecting her children from any danger. My mom was very calm, sweet, patient and caring. She would not get mad easily. Actually, there are just a few times where she would, and it was because my brother and I would fight. Other than that, it was quite hard to see her mad. Now as we were walking the mall, she decided to go into a store named Papaya. If you do not know anything about this store, the name says it all. It is a women's apparel store that only sells women's clothing and accessories. It was during Christmas time, and you know how it gets. Therefore, I told my mother that I would wait for her outside. I was exhausted from walking all over the mall, which you may understand.

As I waited for her, two men in uniform approached me and started to talk to me asking me if I had ever considered joining the army. I remember this distinctly like it was happening right now. As I began to talk with them, my mother rushed out of that Papaya store like I had never seen her. I believe she dropped whatever she had in mind to buy, and told them "My son is not interested, go away". Now, first off, I had never seen my mother run that fast, and secondly, I had never seen my mother so upset. The two officers jetted from that place, and I had to tell my mother to relax because she was agitated. I asked my mother why she had reacted that way, but later I understood that my mother had left El Salvador because of a civil war, and she had seen many of her family members decapitated and experienced her brother being recruited into the government army. She had always talked to us of the atrocities that she lived through. War is not an easy picture that you can erase.

At the same time, I want to thank the women and men that fight for our country's liberty and the sacrifice they make for our families and lives on the battlefront. I have many friends of mine right now who are in the Armed Forces, and I thank them for their sacrifice, commitment and service.

The point that I want to make with this story is how early the Armed Forces look into recruiting. They start to look for young men and women who they see can be a great fit for the Armed Forces. They start enlisting at ages 17 with parental consent, and 18 without parental consent. Ask yourself why? Why so early? Why a 17-year-old? Because if you look at any 17 or 18-year-old, this is a big decision for them. Graduating from high school and then embarking on one of the biggest decisions of your life. This is an age where many 17-year-olds are asking themselves what is next? What do I do from here? The Armed Forces begin to stimulate them to pick the route into a community again where they can belong, cared for, and be loved, but most of all, be remembered. Legacy. Why do the Armed Forces do all this? It is because they see the potential in young people.

These are just two scenarios of distinct groups in society that are both hungry to recruit youth to their teams. First off, they believe in them and surround them with a community, a place where they are loved, cared for, but most of all, belong by making a difference. If you are a young person reading this right now, I want you to realize the potential that is found inside of you And if you are a youth leader, I hope you realize and awaken to the fact that each student in your youth classroom whether 1 or

100 has the potential to do great things. It is time you noticed it, began to believe it, and to speak the words of life from the giver of life into their lives.

CHAPTER 4

EVERYONE HAS A STORY BUT NO ONE HAS YOUR STORY

"Words are how we think, but Stories are how we link"
-Christina Baldwin

Looking back, I use to say I will never, ever, ever be a pastor. I am making sure to emphasize the "Ever" as you can tell. Here is why. During my teenage years, I became a pk. Now if you don't know what that is, it's stands for pretty kid. Just kidding, it stands for preacher's kid. Countless times I would get people coming up to me and saying you will be a preacher like your dad one day. Now you got to understand that is the worst thing you could tell a teenager without ever getting to know them or knowing their aspirations, dreams or even likes and dislikes.

    I grew up with people always telling me you're going be a pastor. That got me mad because people could not see me beyond what my father was. Instead of asking me what I wanted to become, they put me in a box. This happens to many youths today. When they arrive at a church, they are placed in the box of thinking in a certain way, talking a certain way, acting a certain way, and even being a certain way.

Entering college, I was fixated on making $money$, being rich, and I believe many youths pick their professions solely on the possessions they might gain, obtain, or a paycheck that pays well. To a certain extent, I don't point the finger at them and say that is bad, and rather I try to understand their why. It is important always to understand their reasons. That is what led me to study business. It is amazing as I reflect back to see how God was aligning me and preparing me for the mission ahead. Instead, as I was getting older, I began to keep myself away from God. Tell that to my boy Jonah from the Bible. You can't play hide and seek with God. I hit the lowest point in my life being not eligible to return for the next school year at La Sierra University. Because of so many bad choices and decisions I made including partying, clubbing, drinking, smoking, flirting and procrastinating.

As the oldest brother in the family, I was giving the worst example possible to my younger siblings. I had given up on myself. After all that happened to me, I thought to myself, "I am a nobody". But remember God uses the nobodies to show the somebodies. The only description I could give myself was shameful. I told my parents, "you know what dad and mom don't worry about me, I will go to a community college, and just finish there.", I had lost everything, and I had no hope, no faith, no purpose, no passion, no drive, no ambition, no nothing, and I was not being serious about continuing school. I just did not want my parents to be worried about me. I was a total failure. But you've got to understand something. My dad and mama believed in me. They never gave up on me. They said pack your stuff son; you're going to Pacific Union College. I was like "what?" Where is that?

As I entered my second year of college, I was at a new campus, new school, and a new environment. I remember sitting in my dorm room not wanting to leave. I was scared, not knowing anyone is frightening. I could not be stuck in my dorm room forever, so I took the courage to step out of my dorm room, meet a few people, kept partying, drinking, clubbing, smoking, and flirting. You would think that by now, with all that had happened to me, I would have changed. Remember how I said earlier, you cannot play hide and seek with God.

One night I was heading back to my dorm. It was a night like no other; clear sky, and you could see the stars. I had just finished playing basketball. As I was walking up to my dorm, I heard my name, "Jonathan." I looked around thinking it was a friend of mine. I did a 360 roundabout, and no one was near me. I kept walking until I heard my name, "Jonathan." I looked around again, but nothing. I started telling myself this is weird. I hear my name, but no one is around me. As I was close to my dorm, I hear my name again "Jonathan." I look immediately around to see who was calling me, and I realized no one was around me. I looked up. The voice said, "Jonathan, I need you." It hits me hard. This God of the universe had just spoken to me, the worst of sinners. The one who had doubted his name, his power, his love is now calling me. At the moment, I ran straight to my dorm, opened the Bible that I had on my desk but never read and I started to weep uncontrollably. Tears kept coming and dropping on the dusty and dirty pages of the Bible that was on my desk. I could not understand. I felt so unworthy, filthy, but I felt this magnet of love surround me like never before. Love that I did not deserve, a love that took control of me. This quote is a reminder of that experience. Our life is not ours. Our life has been given to us to reflect the SON, to bring glory, and honor to the ONE.

    I believe God has put something in our DNA allowing everyone to have the opportunity to do something amazing. Think about it, what father in this world in his right mind after seeing the face of their son or daughter say to them, "you got no potential, I do see nothing in you that is special." On the contrary, you hold that precious child with arms full of love, and as they continue to grow, you train them, correct them, and most of all, believe in them. You do whatever it takes for that son or daughter of you to understand that they have potential. The Bible says that if we who are evil by nature know how to give good gifts to our children and love them, how much more our Heavenly Daddy loves us.

    There's something huge inside of you. I do not know your age or your story, but I know the ONE who does. He writes the story to fit into HIS story. If you are a youth leader, I believe there are a youths in our youth class that you might have given up on or might have felt like throwing the towel in on their future. But all they need is for you to believe in them, and see them not for who they are, but for what they could become in the hands of our Maker, Creator, GOD. Awaken in them the potential to be led by the Holy Spirit, and to see that life has a purpose.

I get to see that today, so many youths dive into drugs, alcohol, sex & wild parties because they don't see how those small choices can affect and deteriorate their Potential. But I want to tell you they will. The smallest choices you make today will affect and deteriorate the outcome of tomorrow.

Potential, something that I believe God has stored in each human heart that if tapped it, would revolutionize and radicalize not just the church, not just a community, but the WORLD!

CHAPTER 5

SOMETHING HUGE INSIDE OF YOU

"Don't let anybody think that you're too small to set a big example"
-Emmanuel Vendrell (11 years old)

Let me introduce to you my brother Michael who has been underestimated. One time, when I was 19 years old, he shares was at a church in one of the Sabbath school classes, and the teacher (who was one of the elders of the church) was teaching something that was contrary to what the Bible said. So, I raised my hand to share my opinion that I was not in agreement with what he had shared, and I read in the Bible something that was contrary to what he was sharing. He admitted to being wrong, but then started to speak back to me in a very impolite way and said that I was always trying to cause havoc. What he wanted was for me to agree with what he had shared with the group, and just to take what he said only because he was an elder of the church, and I was too young to be confronting him. The reason was not so much about what I said, but it was my appearance; only because I was too young. That is the reason why. We see this same thing take place in the life of David. We will see how he was underestimated only for being young.

The Bible says in 1 Samuel 6 that God speaks to the prophet Samuel and tells him to go to the house of Jesse. God had chosen the son of Jesse to be the next king of Israel and wanted Samuel to anoint him. Samuel arrives at the house of Jesse in verse 6, and Samuel thought that the oldest son Eliab was certain to be the King and said this is certainly the one that God has chosen to be King of Israel.

Then in verse 7, God gives a lesson to all of us human beings. God speaks with Samuel and what strikes me is that God refers to us and tells him not to look at his appearance (his height, his age, his position or his social class) because God was not looking at what the human eyes was seeing. God is not like the human race that only sees the exterior, the appearance, the outward. God looks at the heart.

> "But God told Samuel "Looks aren't everything. Don't be impressed with his looks and stature. I've already eliminated him. God judges a person differently than humans do. Men and women look at the face; God looks into the heart." - 1 Samuel 16:7 (MSG)

We continue reading the story in verse 10. Jesse introducing all his sons to the prophet Samuel, but none of them was chosen. Then Samuel asks Jesse is this it? Are there any more sons? Jesse answers, well there is, but he is the youngest, and he is keeping the sheep safe; pretty much-saying yea he is the youngest one, but he is busy at this moment.

Samuel orders Jesse to get him as he was not leaving from that spot until he saw David, the youngster. Interesting to see how David had no clue what was coming to him at that very instant. He was just fulfilling his daily obligations, and now I could imagine a servant from Jesse comes out screaming from far away asking him to come home immediately. David had not been invited to this special ceremony taking place in his own home. He obviously was not taken into account. Have you ever felt that you're not taken into account by your family? They look at you as the odd one out, our black sheep of the family. They do not take you into account. Imagine how David must have felt? verse 12 says... when the young man came in, God speaks directly to Samuel telling him to get up on his feet! Anoint him! This is the one!

What I love about this is that God values us in spite of our youth, age or experience, and God does not underestimate us. He knows the potential that we have if we place our lives in His Hands. That is why we need to draw close to God so we can know His plans for our lives and reach our maximum potential. So, I encourage you not to be disheartened or discouraged by the obstacles we face in life because it is part of growth, maturity, and serves to push us to achieve something greater in our lives.

Another great story is one of the Philistine giant named Goliath coming in the morning and afternoon for 40 days (the number 40 is biblically numbers of preparation just keep that in mind) challenging the people of Israel. Meaning that for 40 days, God was preparing a brave young man, even though he was underestimated by many because he was young, yet he was not afraid of the challenge.

After 40 days, the giant challenged the Israelite army, but this time it was different because David heard what Goliath said. Then David asked... who is this uncircumcised man who dares challenge the armies of the living God? But when the older brother of David Eliab heard David talking like a man about the situation, he got upset and started to let him know how he needed to be tending the sheep and taking care of his chores at home rather than be in an army camp with all the older trained soldiers. He was pretty much saying you're too young to be here. Go back home and do what you're good at which is tending sheep. Little did Eliab realize the plans God had in mind. What Eliab does not see is that God had given David the preparation necessary to defeat the Giant. Eliab saw the appearance, size, and experience.

The Bible story continues in saying that David was summoned to meet the King of Israel because of the words that he was saying. Saul sent for David, and when David showed up he told the King:

"Do not give up hope. I'm ready to go and fight this Philistine."
- 1 Samuel 17:32 (MSG)

These are the words that came out of King Saul's mouth:

"You can't go and fight this Philistine. You're too young and inexperienced." - 1 Samuel 17:33 (MSG)

Does this sound familiar to your life? Have you experienced something similar to this where people have looked down on you and thought you're too young and inexperienced for the assignment? We see that Saul underestimates David for being too young and inexperienced in combat. He thought David had not been in challenging situations near to death encounters. Look at David's response:

> "I've been a shepherd, tending sheep for my father. Whenever a lion or bear came and took a lamb from the flock, I'd go after it, knock it down, and rescue the lamb...Lion or Bear it made no difference - I killed it. And I'll do the same to this Philistine pig who is taunting the troops of Living God. God, who delivered me from the teeth of the lion and the claws of the bear, will deliver me from this Philistine." 1 Samuel 17:34-37

As I read these words found in God's word, I asked myself to imagine the tone of voice that came with these words. Imagine the posture that David was speaking with when he declared these words in front of the King of Israel. The courage, bravery, valor and nerve to speak this way. That is why it makes sense how Kings Saul's response is short and straight:

"Go, and God help you" - 1 Samuel 17:37

Pretty much saying, hey kid if you want the Giant, he's yours. There are many young men like David today. God has been preparing you to face great challenges ahead, and when the day comes for our great battle opportunity let's be sure never to forget the preparation stage; remembering always that God can take us from Glory to Glory, and from Power to Power. In every moment of our lives, if we continue trusting in God and always looking straight ahead, we will gain the victory.

It continued that when David and Goliath squared up, meaning they faced each other, Goliath underestimated David for being a youngster. There was an audible conversation that took place between David and Goliath. Goliath told him:

> "Am I a dog that you come after me with a stick? And he cursed him by his gods." -1 Samuel 17:43 (MSG)

At that moment, he was not only insulting David but also the God whom David worshipped. He even goes on to say what he was going to do with David's body, feeding it to the birds of the sky and the wild beasts. This is how David answered the Giant Goliath epic moment:

> "You come to me with a sword and spear and battle ax. I come to you in the name of God of the Angel Armies, the God of Israel's troops, whom you have cursed and mocked. This very day God is handing you over to me. I'm about to kill you, cut off your head, and serve up your body and the bodies of your Philistine buddies

to the crows and coyotes. The whole earth will know that there's an extraordinary God in Israel. And everyone gathered here will learn that God doesn't save using sword or spear. The Battle belongs to God- He's handing you to us on a platter!" - 1 Samuel 17:45-47.

Picture yourself in the middle of this dispute. What side are you choosing? Well, many of you already know how the story ends, but what fascinates me and is important to note is that, all through David's early journey, he was underestimated by countless people. Underestimated by those close to him and far from him like his pops (Father), big bro Eliab, King Saul (Leader of a Nation), and Goliath (Israel's worst nightmare) and through it all, God gave him the Victory. In spite of all he had to go through, David knew whose side he was on.

The Bible says David defeated the giant Goliath, and there were huge celebrations and a lot of happiness; all because it happened from the hand of a brave, willing young man, they were able to have the victory.

This is exactly what God is looking for in you and me today. The younger generations of men and women who will fight for what they believe in, hold true to the principles and values that God has placed in their hearts, and ultimately have the faith to know that with God all things are possible. Stop letting the giants in your life intimidate you or drop you, and remember whose corner you are in.

Your heavenly daddy sees you with this amazing potential to do great and mighty things. He does not look at your age, skin color, or your imperfections. He looks straight into your eyes, which are the doors to your heart, and he sees the inner beauty inside you, the gifts inside you, and abilities to do something amazing in this world. What are you waiting for? It is time for you to prepare just like David for the potential opportunity that awaits you.

The Rock. The first person that you and I think about being called the Rock is Dwayne Johnson the wrestler that had his great fame from the WWE and now is an actor, and a producer and at one point maybe you did not know this, but he was a football player. All you've got to do is type in on Google "The Rock", and he is the first person that will appear. But I want to talk to you about the first person who was ever called "The Rock". The original rock.

Want to talk about one of the craziest disciples Jesus recruited in the whole Bible. I know if you have grown up in the church, you might have heard a thing or two about Peter's problem. He had a crazy quick temper. Pick your words wisely around this man or else you might be losing an ear. Peter had a problem. He was outspoken, impulsive, short-tempered, rude, and always took things into his own hands. If there was something wrong, he wanted to be the first to fix it. When people remember Peter, the first things they remember him for is denying Jesus three times, cutting a man's ear or the experience when he walked on water and then drowned because he took his eyes off Jesus.

As I was re-reading Peter's initial beginnings, there was something that hit me like cold water. It is found in John 1:42 where it says that Andrew who was Peter's younger brother brought him to Jesus. Andrew could not think of anyone else more important to bring than his older brother Peter to meet Jesus. I love to imagine for a moment that as Andrew saw Peter, he came jumping, moving uncontrollable and ecstatic to tell his brother whom he had just found: THE MESSIAH. He did not waste time in bringing him to Jesus. He did not say OK we will go tomorrow or I set up an appointment with Jesus next week. For Andrew, it was crucial and imperative that he bring Peter immediately to Jesus. Not another year, week, day, or hour could pass for Peter to meet or encounter THE MESSIAH.

As Andrew brought Peter to Jesus, the Bible says that Jesus looked at him. I want to pause here. Jesus looked at Peter. This was more than just a look. Jesus fixed His eyes on Peter and discerned clearly the path of Peter's life. Jesus' eyes connected with Peter's eyes. They say that the eyes are the window to a person's soul. The Bible says in Matthew 6:22-24, the eyes are the lamp of the body.

In this encounter, Jesus' eyes full of love, full of life and full of light connected with Peter's eyes. Imagine this for a moment; Jesus saw glimpses of Peter's life. He must have seen through Peter's past, problems, temper, shortcomings, but also Jesus saw Peter's potential, who Peter would become in the hands of God. Not who Peter was, but who he would become. Jesus speaks his first words to Peter's life by saying "You are Simon the son of John; you shall be called Cephas which is translated Peter Rock" pretty much saying I know who you are Peter, but I also know who you will become. Jesus saw Peter's potential. He breathed into Peter's life words of life that would radically change his life.

Now, would Peter after Jesus said these powerful words have shortcomings and downfalls? Off course yes, he would have many times where he did not understand a clue about what Jesus said or did, he would drown in the water, cut an ear, reject his friend Jesus, and go back to fishing. And it would take him a couple of years to finally get it and understand those initial first words Jesus had declared about Peter's potential. But after all of this had occurred in Peter's life and after Jesus had died and resurrected, Jesus knows that Peter is devastated, disappointed and depressed by what he had just done in denying and rejecting his friend Jesus. In John 21 Jesus goes out of his way and searches again for Peter. Jesus could have begun with how most human beings would begin this conversation, why did you deny me? How could you reject me in front of everyone? I thought you were my friend. But look at how Jesus begins this conversation "Si-mon son of John, do you love me... more than these?" WHAAAT…… This is mind-blowing.

Jesus, by asking Peter, led him through an experience that would remove one of the darkest and guiltiest moments in Peter's life. Peter had denied Jesus three times, and now Jesus was making Peter aware of his potential that even though his past is full of guilt, shame, denial and problems, he would still fulfill his promise to Peter being a rock and use his potential to lead the greatest movement of salvation on planet earth.

Jesus saw something in Peter that Peter did not see in himself, the potential to do great things for the Kingdom Life. Later on, we continue reading how Peter is filled with the power of the Holy Spirit in Acts 2:14 preaching, and at once there was added about 3,000 souls.

Just like Peter, you and many youth around you have the God gifted and given potential to do powerful things for God's Kingdom.

PART 2: PERSPECTIVE

Sometimes, God doesn't change your situation because He is trying to change your perspective.

Perspective is a way of seeing life despite all life's problems, circumstances or outcomes.

Perspective is what keeps us focused on the positive things in the worst situations.

Perspective is what helps you see beyond the problem to place your complete dependence and trust in the Ultimate Planner God.

CHAPTER 6

PICTURE PERSPECTIVE

There is more to a picture than what you initially see.
There is more to a youth than what you first perceive.

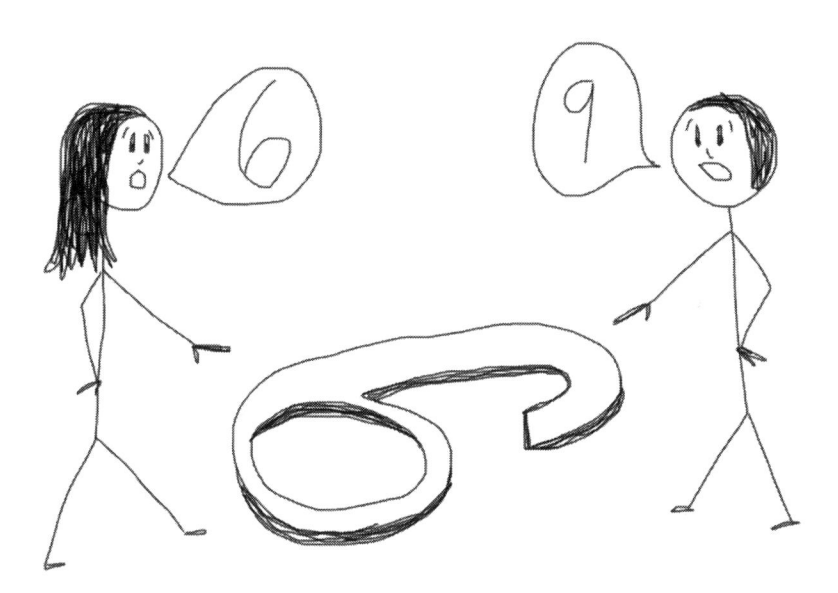

Don't you just love this sunset... it's perfect.

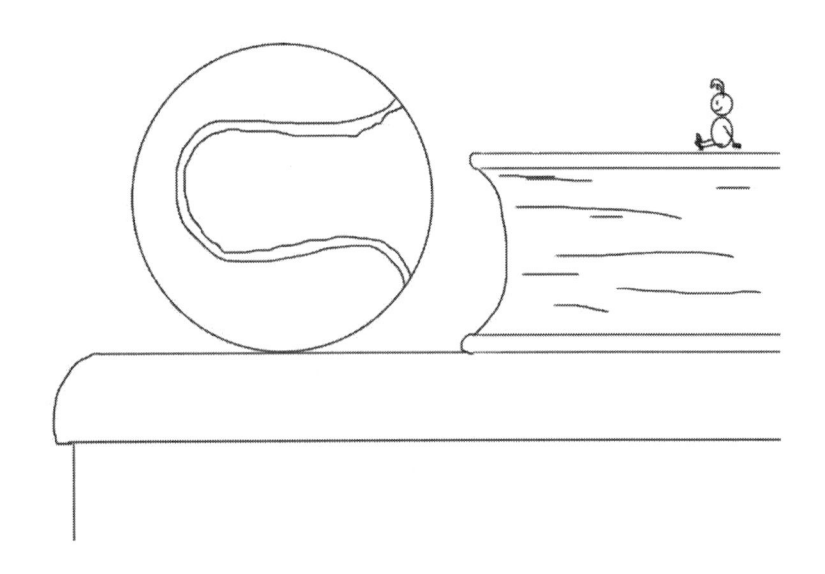

CHAPTER 7

FROM SURROUNDED TO GROUNDED

"Happiness is not the absence of problems, it's the ability to see pass them."

"Sometimes, God doesn't change your situation because He is trying to change Your Perspective"

I am hyped to tell you about this story. It's one of my favorite stories in the Bible and comes from the era of the Kings of Israel. In 2nd Kings 6, it tells us the biblical story of a prophet named Elisha who was in life and death situation. The prophet Elisha was surrounded by enemies who wanted to destroy him. You might be asking why? What did Elisha do? Well, you've got to understand that Elisha was a Prophet (God's mouthpiece) and would tell the King of Israel all of the secrets and strategies of the King of Aram. Could you imagine you're the King of Aram planning the next ambush attack or tactic and next thing you know the opposition knows exactly what you were going to do, even the whispers in your bedroom? Mercy. That's intense.

The King of Aram sent his whole army and came by night to surround the city. Have you ever felt surrounded by the enemy? Surrounded by fear? Surrounded by failure? Felt outnumbered? The odds are against you. Could you imagine waking up to a morning and seeing yourself surrounded and outnumbered? This is exactly what was going on in the life of the servant of Elisha. He goes on to say what any of us would have said: "What shall we do?" Check out Elisha's response:

> He said, "Don't worry about it; there are more on our side than on their side." Then Elisha prayed, "Oh God, open his eyes and let him see" The eyes of the young man were opened, and he saw. A Wonder! The whole mountainside is full of horses and chariots of fire surrounding Elisha! - (2 Kings 6:16-17)

In this story, we can see how the prophet Elisha and his servant are in the same situation, but there is a big difference in their perspective. One sees something different than what the other sees. One is scared for his life, while the other is calm and composed. One is ready to surrender to the King of Aram, and one is surrendered totally to the King of Kings and Lord of Lord to the God of Angel Armies. One is shaking in fear and frightened; while the other is saying "Bring it" I know who is for me. Two very contrasting perspectives both are facing the same problem.

This happens to us many times in our lives where we are in difficult situations, and just like the servant of Elisha, we only look at what lies in front of us. The situation, the problem, the hardship, the difficulty, the impossible which I believe handicaps us from seeing the heavenly perspective of the situation. This is where it is important to see who we turn to in this crisis moment. We see Elisha said a prayer asking God to open his servant's eyes. This is where I believe prayer is the avenue that unleashes the aid of Heaven at our hand. Elisha saw something that his servant had not yet seen, but once Elisha prayed for his servant, he was able to see the battalion of angels ready for attack. Wow! Think about this for a moment. Just when you think your life was done, you look again and see you are being protected. Prayer helps us see the problem from a different perspective. One of my favorite quotes about prayer says, "God can do more in one moment that we could ever do in a lifetime." That is why I pray.

This was the moment that changed the servant's perspective forever. I do not believe you forget an experience like that one. It leaves a spiritual reminder for life. A reminder that there are more on your side than you once thought. It reminds me of the song by Chris Tomlin "Whom Shall I fear" (Check out the song), and also reminds me of a Bible text:

For God has not given us a spirit of fear and timidity, but of power, love and self-discipline. So never be ashamed to tell others about our Lord. (2 Timothy 1:7-8)

Also, Romans 8:31 If God be for us who can be against us. Pretty much saying, who fights for us and is on our side is God, so we encourage you to have a different perspective about your situation keeping in mind that God is on our side, and there is a saying that I always need to remind myself and maybe you can as well "Do not tell God how big your problem is, tell your problem how big your God is."

CHAPTER 8

PERSCRIBED PERSPECTIVE

When Life Gets Blurry, Adjust your Focus.

Through what lens do you see life? What is your perspective on life? At the end of the year, I have a bad habit. What I do is line up all my doctor appointments including ophthalmologist, dentist, and physicians. As you well know at the end of the year, the insurances start a new cycle, and whatever you did not use in terms of your benefits, you end up losing them. I bet you knew that because I have seen how at the end of the year the lines get crazy. It will be a miracle if you get an appointment.

    Just a couple of weeks ago, I decided to go to the ophthalmologist to get an eye exam. Can I keep it real with you all? Is that a yes... sure... ok... please do not tell anyone, but I love glasses. I should only use them for reading, but I am always wearing them. You might be asking why? I think they make you look more sophisticated and handsome, just saying. Anyways, as the eye doctor took a look at me and began doing the test, she asked me to read the letters and numbers on the chart. She then put this huge machine over my eyes and told me to let her know which lens I saw more clearly with one or two. I told her one, and then she asked me three or four. I was a bit confused and asked her, "I thought you had just told me either one or two. Why three or four?" and she said because it helps me know what exact prescription you will be needing. The machine allows the light to bend properly when it passes through the cornea and retina of your eye. The machine is called a Phoropter and determines the prescription you will be using.

This got me thinking, if it was not for that Phoropter machine, where my eyes were located as she was switching the lenses, I would never know exactly my prescription, and what precise lenses I would need to see correctly and clearly.

Our eyes are everything to us. Think about it, without them we would have a hard time getting from place to place. In this life, you know that we need a Phoropter to be able to provide us with a prescription to see clearly and correctly in this world. I believe with all my heart; the Phoropter is the Word of God. The Bible identifies whose we are, who we are, and where we come from, Identity, Purpose, and belonging. It lights not only our eyes but our lives. It gives you more than a prescription; it gives a perspective about life. There is no better doctor to trust and run these eye exams than the originator of your life, Jesus. I love this verse in Hebrews 4:12.

"For the Word of God is alive and active, it is sharper than a double-edged sword, cutting between the soul and the spirit, cutting between joint and marrow. It exposes our innermost thoughts and desires."

The word of God leaves you exposed to who you really are. Just like the eye test tells you exactly what kind of prescription you need.

But you know what many of us do instead; we look for the alternative way out. We look for shortcuts. We look for the easy way out, like buying glasses without a prescription or trying on someone else's glasses. The last time I tried on my friend's glasses, my vision went blurry quickly.

This can be applied to each one of our lives. We see things from other people's perspective without ever evaluating or going to the eye doctor to get the real prescription. Many of us use other prescription lenses and see through their perspective without ever evaluating their intentions. It is time to re-check our perspective. It is time to have a perspective that aligns with the vine. Let me explain.

The bible says, "I am the vine and you are the branches… remain in me and I in you" Let me take you back to when Jesus said these words. It was His last moments on planet earth. His time had come. He was about to depart. I do not know about you, but I hate goodbyes. I hate dropping loved ones at the airport and not knowing when will be the next time we will be reunited. It has happened to me several times with my family. It has gotten to the point that as I am dropping them off, I begin sobbing uncontrollably. As human beings, we all have at one point, or another dropped off a person that was dear to us, that we loved with all our heart, and it was hard to say goodbye.

This was exactly what was going on with Jesus and his disciples. It was time. Time to fulfill the greatest mission the world could ever imagine or experience or contemplate. The whole universe was on their feet to see how this earth was going to be redeemed. Jesus had some final words he wanted to leave with his disciples, his friends. He said; "Yes, I am the Vine; you are the branches. Those who remain in me, and I in them, will produce much fruit. For apart from me you can do nothing." - John 15:5.

A perspective that is aligned with the vine from Jesus' own words. What strikes me the most is the last sentence "apart from me you can do nothing." It hits me. This means if we do not stay connected, glued, attached, and linked up with Jesus, we can do NO-Thing. Anything. Nada. Many of you might be thinking, well I have done many things with Jesus out of the picture. Yes, you have, but the Bible is clear that apart from Jesus, you cannot produce fruits. Think about it this way. Imagine a life alone, no friends, no family, no relationships with anyone. How do you envision that life? When you want to share your experience of school or work with someone, there is no one to share it with. When you want to laugh with someone, cry with someone, or even hug someone, there is no one around. Just complete loneliness. This will produce insecurity, fear, doubt and many other feelings just by living a lonely life. Now imagine living life with your best friend. Laughing, talking, cooking, and playing together. It's a completely different life. This is the same thing here, Jesus is saying that, with Jesus, life is more meaningful, and if you take up His perspective of staying connected with Him, you will experience a completely whole life full of fruits. The bible says:

The fruits of the Spirit are love, joy, peace, patience, kindness, faithfulness, gentleness and self-control against these there is no law. - Galatians 5:22-23.

Since I have understood this one verse, it has changed and revolutionized my perspective. Because at the end of the day, it is through whose lenses or through whose perspective you see life through. As I align my life with Jesus, I start to see things from the creator's lenses and start to experience love, joy, peace, patience, kindness, faithfulness, gentleness and self-control. I'm telling you to try it, read His Word, and start to see life in a new way, full of love, full of identity, full of belonging, full of purpose, full of a perspective that is prescribed by the true physician.

CHAPTER 9

YOU GOT THIS!

We spend so much time focusing on the problem that we can't see past a solution. It's time for a shift in your Perspective.

As I sat down here, in PUC after five years, I found myself sitting in the girl's dorm. You might be asking me...what are you doing in a girl's dorm? Let me make it clear. I was sitting down in a girl's lobby waiting for my wife to come down with my sister. All of a sudden, I began to listen to someone else's conversation. I know exactly what you are thinking, this nosy pastor. Alright, I will admit I was nosy, and I shouldn't, but let me tell you, this girl entering the dorm hall was loud. Could not help it. This girl comes into the lobby receptionist and starts pouring her frustration about how her computer updates have ruined her day. She cannot get anything done. Oh, this is it; she will be failing this semester. She has had enough, and this is it. I turned to the receptionist to see how she would react. To my surprise, the receptionist was so kind and empathetic by offering to see the positive in the situation and provide solutions to her problem like going to the library and using one of the computers there. Which to me hearing this sounded like a great idea, but this girl kept rambling about the how's. How her computer was acting up, how she kept dropping things that day, how she has so much homework, how she would have to be up till 3 am, how life isn't fair, and how her test was going to be hard.

It amazing to see how the receptionist handled the problem by saying you know what, I have a huge test coming up too, let's make a deal. Let's use this time to study for our test. How does that sound? So, we are being productive with our day. We can do this Girl! As I was listening and watching this conversation unfolding, I thought to myself that is not going to work, I bet she is going to continue to ramble and fuss about her problem, but to my surprise, that girl became excited and stoked. She said, "Let's do this" followed by a high five. She became fueled by what someone else was going through, what she was going through & was energized by it.

"You can do this" were the words that the girl who once was nagging and making excuses was sharing with someone else that came into the dorm stressed out.

Have you met people that just seem to share their excuses and frustrations with everyone else? Problems are just constantly surrounding them, and you get to hear them all the time. Or you might be that person that battles through many problems and share them with your friends or in some cases with everyone you come in contact with. Let me tell you, problems are a part of life, but you knew that already.

Instead of focusing on the problem, I believe not only our youth leaders, but every person needs to check their perspective. I love the quote that says, "you can't change your problem, but you can change your perspective". Problems will come. That's inevitable. Problems will arise from inside or outside. But imagine if you were to let your perspective dictate and drive the problems in your life. For example, you got an F on your Test, or your car got a flat tire on the road. These situations can cause you to nag, whine, and complain or can build character and learn from these moments. Have you noticed as human beings, we derive the best stories to share with others from the most embarrassing, draining, catastrophic events and we lived to tell the story.

    Want to finish with this. About a year ago, I watched the movie "Unbroken." The word that kept ringing in my head throughout the movie was perseverance. If you have not watched it, let me just give you a little about it, so you get where I'm trying to go. I promise I will not spoil the whole movie. Personally, I do not like people spoiling movies because I know how it feels. It is a true story about Louis "Louie" Zamperini a young boy that has its roots in an Italian family that made its way to America. At an early age, he's careless about life. No direction, no purpose, being bullied and called all sorts of names. He begins to act "wild" robbing, drinking, and smoking and even became a troublemaker. As the movie starts to unfold, you would think this young boy has no future, no purpose, and no direction of where he is going. Many people would throw this boy's potential out the window, but as his older brother starts to see that Louie his younger sneaks to track, meets and starts to discover his enjoyment to run. The one thing he enjoys doing, that one thing he is passionate about, but the problem lies in that Louie does not think he has neither the potential nor the perspective to run with the other kids. He checks out of the race before the race has even begun. I believe many youths check out for their potential and perspective before they even have begun to warm up. They say I can't do it, and I'm too young, I'm too slow, I'm too... (You finish the sentence).

But there is something that changes the trajectory of Louie's life. His brother believes in him. I am here to tell you all it takes is for one person to believe in you. One person to believe in the youth that God has given you. All it takes is one, that one I believe is you. His brother was the first to believe in him. First to see something in him that he had not yet seen in himself. His brother says to him if you keep going the way you're going, you will end up as a bum in the street, but if you fight harder than those other guys and train, you will win. "You can do this Louie, and you just got to believe you can." The next nine words that his brother says to his brother's life catapult him to reaching milestones that he would never have imagined. He said, "If you can take it, you can make it." That belief launched his entire life, and through his brother's words, it infused life, and he recognized and realized there is one person that believes "I can." Louie becomes not only an Olympic athlete but a prisoner of war. And throughout the movie, you see that the words his brother spoke to him on that day brought about an inspired life. By this one person believing in his Potential, helping him see a new perspective in the midst of this problem, it brought about Perseverance in Louie's life.

I am here to remind you the Word of Life says, "I can do all things through Christ who gives me strength." You can; I can, we can do all things through Christ who enables us to continue and give us the energy to continue. Pretty much Jesus is telling you "You got this."

CHAPTER 10

YOUR CONNECTIONS INFLUENCE YOUR DIRECTION

"To find peace, you have to be willing to lose your connection with the people, places and things that create all the noise in your life."

Think about this, who are the people that you are connected or surrounded by at this moment? Who do you spend most of your time with? Identify their names? Think about their aspirations and motivations. What are they after? What drives them? Who are they being influenced by? What are the conversations that you mostly have with these people? What do you guys mainly do together? The reason I ask these questions is that whoever you are connected or surrounded by will influence and drive your perspective.

I love to think that some people have injected me with faith, with their sayings and influenced me to be someone, and see life from another perspective. I believe that life is a struggle of influences that build up or break down, but I think our influence as sons or daughters of God should be built on the power Jesus gave us to build, and influence others to be part of the movement.

Jesus knew about the power of influence. Look at how one time in the Bible there was a widow who had lost her only son. Could you imagine a mother losing her son? One of the tough things about being a Pastor for me has been funerals. Just seeing humans break down and cry, torn by the loss of their loved one. I have witnessed a daughter losing her father whispering in his ear "daddy wake up, wake up daddy, let us go home" to a youth of mine losing her grandfather "Papa" as she caresses his hair. Now the toughest funeral I had to perform was a mother losing two of her children. This mother was broken, she could not even walk, she yelled at the top of her lungs longing to be able to hold her two children. It is one of the hardest things I have witnessed. How do you console or comfort a mother? Now we go back to Luke 7 verse 11 where a mother had lost her husband, and now lost the only thing left in her life which was her son. Life was just sucked out of her. Now picture yourself walking in as a disciple of Jesus with this funeral procession walking out of the town. A large crowd followed this mother to show her support, and console her in this horrendous moment. The Bible says that when the Lord saw her, his heart overflowed with compassion. The first words Jesus utters to this mother was "Don't Cry." Then the Bible says Jesus walked towards the coffin and touched it. Stop. Halt. Wait. WHAT... Jesus touched the coffin. Now, first of all, you have to understand that in those days, the moment a clean person touched something unclean you would automatically become unclean. That was the law. Everyone knew this. The representation of Jesus touching the coffin would have caused many of the crowd who were there consoling the mother to be in shock. This was the law. This is something that was taught. Now imagine what this shock meant to all the people who were present, a man who just walked into their town and told a woman, a mother who has lost it all, not to cry. I bet there was a lot of bickering and whispering coming from the crowd. Come on. Comments like "who does this man think he is," "how dare he tell this mother to stop crying" "doesn't he realize that this mother just lost her only son" "wait, what is he doing now" "he is touching the coffin" "unclean" "he is unclean." As the crowd murmurs and the bearers stop, Jesus utters his next words as his hands are touching the coffin, a representation of clean with unclean he says, "young man, I tell you to get up." Not only a touch, but the words of life were spoken to this young man's life. The same words that spoke this world into existence were the same words that brought this young man back to life. Boom. Breathe in his Nostrils, the breath of life. Whooooo. The boy stood up and began to talk. What would you have done if the next thing you noticed was a man standing up from a coffin? People were shocked and astonished by this miracle. The Bible continues saying that great fear swept the crowd and they praised God saying, "A mighty prophet has risen among us" "God has visited his people today" News about Jesus spread like wildfire.

    Influences create wildfires. The crowd went from a funeral procession to a connection with the Creator. All because a man named Jesus was walking into the town and saw a mother broken by the death of her child. Moved by compassion. Let me break this word compassion down a little. Since one of my professors shared this thought with me, I believe it would be right for me to share it with you. The word compassion means that his inner organs were moved. As he saw her heart, a mother's heart, his heart felt what she felt. His organs were connected with what her organs were feeling. Jesus knew exactly what she was going through. Jesus could not pass this mother by. He knew she was crushed emotionally, spiritually and physically. She was in anguish, and Jesus not only saw it but felt it. Wow, what a Creator we have that can empathize with our sufferings. Now, going back to this point on influence, you've got to understand the power of it. This was an event that began the day with cries, clamor, and sadness, and because of Jesus influence and connection, he was able to turn it around to a joyful, exuberant, and celebration of life. The Bible in Romans 8:11:

> The Spirit of God, who raised Jesus from the dead, lives in you. And just as God raised Christ Jesus from the dead, he will give life to your mortal bodies by this same Spirit living within you.

I believe that God has given us that power and authority to speak words of life that may influence others to experience an everlasting life. Your words have the power to encourage or discourage. Your life has the power to impact someone else's life. Your smile has the impact on someone else's smile. Look at what Jeremiah 15:19,

> This is how the LORD responds: "If you return to me, I will restore you so you can continue to serve me. If you speak good words

rather than worthless ones, you will be my spokesman. You must influence them; do not let them influence you!

What strikes me most about the life of Jesus which is found in the Gospels, especially in the book of John, how over and over again when a person had a personal encounter or connections with Jesus, He would offer them a new perspective on life. Jesus did it for Nicodemus, a respected religious leader seeking answers to his questions in the late hours of the night. Jesus did it for a Samaritan woman who went to a well to refill her water supply, yet unexpectedly, encounters the Son of God and is offered living water. Jesus did it for his disciples. After bringing them food and asking them to eat, Jesus tells them my food is to do the will of my Father who sent me and accomplish the salvation of the world and empower you to carry the work. That is my true nourishment and fulfillment. This was Jesus power bar. This was his protein shake. This is what infused him to keep going.

Jesus was on a mission. Every chance He had to connect to the human heart, He wanted to show them a new perspective on life. A heavenly perspective to see past our problems, past our circumstances, past our afflictions, past our fears, past our insecurities, past this world, and to see the kingdom life. Many times, he said the Kingdom of God is like a mustard seed. Other times he said it was like fishing net, but all in the sum of reminding us the kingdom life is connected with us as long as we are connected to Christ, and through that connection, we can influence the world.

CHAPTER 11

A CRAZY PERSPECTIVE

Learn to see Life from God's Point of View

So I am a little bit out there when it comes to not being shy. I have no problem asking random people questions about anything and everything. So in this instance, I asked several people to give me the first name that popped into their head when they have a crazy thought. But before I give you the answers of what some of them said I would like to know what your answer to this question is:

When you think of crazy who is the first person that comes to your mind? Why?

When I think of someone who was in the Bible that was crazy, I think of Paul. Let me explain before you erase me from your church or start calling me names. First off, Paul had a crazy life, and through his circumstances, he radically adopted crazy perspective. He went from one extreme to the other. Now if you have never known much about him, let me give you a little background. So before he became Paul, his name was

Saul of Tarsus which is a combination of who he was and where he was from. Especially when you have so many Saul or famous names. It is cool because people know where you're from. Anyways, from an early age, Saul of Tarsus had witnessed how the Jewish leaders stoned these so-called Christians. He had witnessed the stoning of Stephen, and the Bible records that Saul was like the one taking care of the coats of these furious Jewish leaders. He must have been young or still under training that he had to watch the coats. It just reminds me of how in sports they have the rookies carrying, watching, and lifting all the equipment. That was Saul's role while he was still under training, he was not allowed yet to be part of the actions, but he observed how the Jewish leaders acted upon the follower of the way.

They were so mad that they had to take off their coats to stone this man. Mercy. Lord Help us. Can you believe that? The Bible says in Acts 8 that Saul was one of the witnesses and he grew up with this hatred and anger towards the Christians and wanted to destroy the church. He only hated them because that was what he was taught from an early age. All he knew growing up was how these Jewish leaders wanted to eliminate these followers of Jesus. Can you believe that? So, hatred only begets hatred, and that is exactly what drove Saul of Tarsus to go after the Christians. These Jewish leaders had influenced his perspective on life, and they had engraved this idea in his mind. The enemies were the Christians, and it was their mission to kill and destroy them. Wow. Talk about hate. Talk about raising a tyrant. Talk about the atrocities this man had witnessed. Talk about what the Jewish leaders had created in the person of Saul of Tarsus. Killing at all cost. This was influence from people who were thought to be the religious leaders of the day. The ones known to have the strongest connection with the heavenly Father. Can you believe this? The only thing on Saul of Tarsus' mind was to wipe out the followers of The Way. In Acts 9:1, "Meanwhile, Saul was uttering threats in every breath, and eager to kill the Lord's followers."

Saul of Tarsus, the man on a mission. He was carrying out what he thought he was born to do. Until one day on the road to Damascus, his life changed forever. It hits me, and I want you to know: a man's mission is not God's mission. God had to interrupt Saul's mission and his plans. The light of the world reached down to one of the dictators of the day and threw him to the ground. Then a voice from heaven said:

> "Saul, Saul, why are you persecuting me? I am Jesus, the one you are persecuting! Now get up and go into the city, and you will be told what you must do."

Jesus own words, the Son of God. Saul was blinded; it got me thinking sometimes God has to blind you for you to reflect, but most of all to cry out to Him. A turning point. When you are in a helpless situation, the first thing we turn to is God for help. I know there have been many times in my life that I have called and cried out to God for help especially being in pastoral ministry. Saul's eyes were completely shut off, turned off. This is where I believe God was downloading the plans and visions and places, but most of all, the heavenly perspective. God had a plan for the life of Saul. Look what he says:

> Go, for Saul is my chosen instrument to take my message to the Gentiles and kings, as well as to the people of Israel. And I will show him how much he has to suffer for my name sake.

This is where he had a shift in his perspective. Think about it. Just like the song Amazing Grace says "I once was blind, but now I see" that was the turning point in Paul's perspective.

Look how Paul would see things after he was all in for God. In Romans 5:3-5

> We can rejoice, too, when we run into problems and trials, for we know that they help us develop endurance. And endurance develops strength of character, and character strengthens our confident hope of salvation. And this hope will not lead to disappointment. For we know how dearly God loves us because he has given us the Holy Spirit to fill our hearts with his love.

Power pack verse right here. Let me unpack it a little. Paul has come to a point in his life where instead of regret, reacting or taking revenge on the people; he is rejoicing and glorifying God. The reason Paul implies this is not because he is a freak. Not because he loved being whipped or being imprisoned, but he understands that all this is helping him become who God wants him to be. This verse also talks about difficult situations, but the perspective of Paul is not the trials, but it is what the trials are producing or developing in him. He must have asked himself why is this all happening to me? Just like many youths are asking themselves why is my father not in my life? Why did God take my mother so early? Why have my parents separated? There are times where we as human beings have a hard time understanding what these trials or difficulties in our lives are producing inside us. And I would like for us to take some time and focus for a little on the word produce. Produce has many definitions, but in the original language which is Greek, the word in the text is "katergazomai" which means to work out, to effect, or to bring out, as a result, to fabricate or elaborate a substance that is useful for oneself. Meaning that, the hard times in our lives develop a substance in our lives which is patience. Think about it, patience is the attitude that leads the human being to be able to endure setbacks and difficulties to develop a better character. For me, I believe that patience is the attitude that makes us see our difficult situations from a positive perspective. The verse follows saying that patience produces proof and the test produces hope. The meaning of hope is an optimistic state of mind in which we desire or aspire to see the possibilities. I have learned in all this that the difficult situations in our lives produce in us things that make us stronger to achieve our dreams and be an inspiration to this generation.

    Another verse that I would like to share with you is 2 Corinthians 4:17 which say: For this light, momentary affliction is preparing for us an eternal weight of glory beyond all comparison. I love it when it says this momentary slight tribulation. The perspective of Paul of the tribulation that was going on in his life was something momentary, short, something that ends, something that is not forever, but what produces the tribulation is something eternal, something that does not pass, something that is forever. The eternal weight of glory.

PART 3: POSITION

A Position is a place that is not permanent; we will always go about changing positions in life whether it is at school, at work, at home or in our society. The important thing is to learn in each of those positions how to be a better person, and how to be able to serve others because remember that Jesus came to earth not to be served but to serve.

God will position you in distinctive places all for service. Position is acknowledging where you are in life and allowing God to work through you for His greater purpose.

CHAPTER 12

CLEANING TOILETS

God will position you in particular places during distinctive seasons to prepare you for His ultimate plan & purpose.

You won't believe it, but my first job in college as a freshman was the janitor of the lady's dormitory. Now, the first couple weeks was fun being a janitor of the lady's dormitory. Here's why, because I went to a college that no women or men were allowed beyond a checkpoint in respective dormitories. But being that I was a staff and worked in the ladies residential hall guess what? I could go beyond the checkpoint. I remember on one occasion, I was hanging with my friends, and suddenly, they saw me go beyond the check-point where men were prohibited from passing. They looked at me frightened and shocked that I had crossed the line, and they were waiting for the residential dean to get my attention, but what they did not know is that I had full access. And when they figured out my all-access passes, they were like that's cool, you get to go behind enemy lines and see the girl's dorm. Anyways that thrill lasted for a short while because, at first like any job, you are thrilled & excited to be working and you're getting to know everyone but then after the first month, reality kicks in.

Did it ever happen to you that as you are getting ready to go to work, your friends decide to plan the most entertaining event or decide to go out and hang out, but now you're stuck with the decision to either go to work or hang out with your friends? To go out and enjoy a great time or to clean toilets in the girl's dorm. It was hard because I had given my supervisor my word. That job taught me a lot about the importance of the particular position in a determined season.

It's interesting as I look back at the several positions God placed me in, and many of them were a janitor position. I cleaned a lot of toilets, staircases, vacuumed and it's interesting how looking back God was preparing me for different future experiences. From a janitor, God took me to be an Assistant RA (Residence Assistant) for the dorm, a little promotion. To then taking on an internship accountant position in a fancy resort which I've got to say it was all God. I mean it was all God because I was the worst student in my class, and then became an assistant accountant in a resort to later during my Masters. I was the gym coordinator and then taking on the assistant coaching position for both soccer and basketball to finally becoming a youth pastor where I am currently at.

As I look back, it is amazing to see how God was preparing me for every season of my life for the ultimate plan and purpose He has for me as I believe he has for you. I can't say I have finally arrived. Many would say being a pastor you have arrived, but what I can say is that up to this point, God has been there! He knows what's next.

When we check out Joseph's life, he was also in different places and positions in his life that formed him and shaped him into where God ultimately wanted to take him.

Joseph went through the pit position. This position is one that many don't want to experience because being in a pit position is one that is messy and dirty. It's one where you feel alone and helpless. Pit position is one where you see no solution. You feel like that is where you will be for the rest of your life. Darkness and dirt surround you, and as you look around, you can only see despair. This could be that 5 am-5 pm job where you are working your butt off. You work and work and seem like you are going nowhere. You wake up, go to work, and come back to find yourself in the next morning. Or you might be one who wakes up heads to work and then finds yourself a couple of hours later at another job just wanting to survive. Just wanting to stay afloat, just in survival mode. Life for you is just about survival. You keep at it, trying to get out of that hole in which you find yourself, and as you keep trying to climb out, you are brought down again and again. You're tired, defeated, worn out, and you are running on empty. The Bible says in Genesis 37:24 the pit was empty. I want you to know you are not alone. I felt the same way, and Joseph must have felt the same way too. You might be asking how did he get out a pit position? Joseph knew that God was with him. One day, as there was a caravan of merchants coming by, one of Joseph's brothers Judah gave the idea that instead of killing him, sell him. Therefore, Joseph was on his way from a pit position to being sold as a slave. He went from being a son of Jacob to be a slave all in one day. Imagine how Joseph must have been feeling?

Right after Joseph was taken out of the pit position, he was sold to the merchants and later bought by Potiphar and was promoted and just when you think things are looking great for Joseph, Potiphar's wife plays Joseph by wanting to sleep with him. And because Joseph had a perspective that was in line with the vine, meaning he knew the Lord was with him and knew that was a great sin in God's sight, the only solution out was to run far away. This was a great scandal that landed Joseph in another position which resulted in the prison position. Put yourself for a minute in Joseph shoes knowing you did the right thing at the right time at the right moment but still are blamed for it and punished for something you know you did not commit. Has it ever happened to you, that by telling the truth you are treated as guilty? Deep down inside, you know it is not your fault that you should not be in the position which you find yourself. Now Joseph found himself inside a prison cell, locked up. Imagine after finding yourself in the best promotional position to later be hit with the news you are going to jail for something you know deep down inside you did not commit. This is the story of Joseph, and it might be your story. It must have been heartbreaking. Just when you think you were making it, just when you think things were looking brighter, just when you can see things were lightening up you feel the chains being wrapped around your arms and legs, and being taken to your prison cell with other criminals and convicts, making you one of them. I believe there are many today in the prison position. The prison position is one that has a prisoner wrapped and trapped. It has a prisoner trapped in the prison of fears, prison full of insecurities, prison full of regrets, prison full of failures, prison full of shame, prison full of guilt, prison full of worries, prison full of the past, prison full of lies, prison full of drugs, prison full of pain, and prison full of all kinds of problems. But what I love is Genesis 39:21, that when Joseph was placed in the prison position, the Bible says, "But the LORD was with Joseph and showed him everlasting love and gave him favor in the sight of the keeper of the prison." Perspective to know that despite the prison cell, the LORD was with Joseph and the Lord is with you. You heard me right God is still with you. He will not only be with you but position people in your life whom can impact your life as well as you can influence theirs. God's love will penetrate the prison cells, and make you see things from a different perspective. Rather than looking at the prison full of problems, you will look at the prison full of opportunities. I love this quote by Walter E. Cole who says, "If we are to achieve a victorious standard of living today, we must look for the opportunity in every difficulty instead of being paralyzed at the thought of the difficulty in every opportunity." That is exactly what Joseph did. Joseph became in charge of the prisoners. He was doing prison ministry as a prisoner himself. He looked at the opportunities right in front of him rather than allowing time and energy to let the prison dictate his life. Because of his prison ministry, Joseph knew the gift God had given him which was interpreting the dream which he did for the cupbearer and the baker. This gave Joseph the opportunity later on when Pharaoh had a dream, and no one could interpret his dream. Then the cupbearer remembered how Joseph could interpret dreams.

In all that Joseph did, he always placed God as a priority in his life, no matter the position in his life. He lived a life devoted to serving God. I believe the moment we can realize this in our own lives and apply it in every context is when we will acknowledge God's power to position us in places for His greater purpose. After Joseph interpreted Pharaoh's dream, he put him in charge as second in command of all of Egypt. Talk about a huge promotion. I can imagine the headline on the Egyptian news for that day "from a prison to the palace".

A palace is a place where many of us want to begin. We want the position of the palace. We believe the palace position will bring us pleasure, power and prestige. But what Joseph had that Pharaoh saw in him was not a hunger for pleasure, power or prestige, but rather the Spirit of God living in him and Pharaoh could not think of anyone more qualified and full of wisdom than Joseph. Therefore, Joseph was placed in the palace position with a purpose to prepare the people of Egypt, but also to assist his family, God's people, during this great famine. Imagine the impact and reaches that Joseph a man of God had not only on his family, not only on his brothers who had betrayed him but also a nation. It was evident that God was on Joseph's side. I love what Joseph said at the end of their reconciliation to his brothers, "what you meant for evil, God meant for good." Remember that what people meant for evil, God can turn it around and build it for the greater good.

CHAPTER 13

WHERE HAVE YOU BEEN POSITIONED?

Every Position is just a transition

Reflect on your Journey through Life. What positions have you had? Think back to your first positions whether at church, school or work?

Write them below:

1. _____
2. _____
3. _____
4. _____
5. _____

It is interesting as you have filled out some of the positions what, have you noticed? Any trends? Any growth? How have these positions prepared you? What have you learned?

We live in a society that places a lot of importance on the job position. Imagine with me for a moment that you are unemployed, and you are seeking a job position. Now the first thing in any job interview, the most important thing that they want to see from you is your resume. Why? Because the resume gives them a little about who you are, what you can bring to the company, what you have accomplished, your experience, and what prior job positions you have had that have prepared you to take up this new job position.

It is important to reflect where you have been positioned. Many times, we never sit back to realize the position that we have been placed in. We get caught up in the next promotion and never reflect on our positioning, how far we have come, what have we learned, what skills have we acquired. We become so focused on what is next rather than taking the time to see what you have learned through the transitions.

Therefore, let me tell you if you are not in the right position, you will never be able to manifest your full potential. Let me simply illustrate this. Michael and I signed up to play in a basketball league on Wednesday nights, and as we began to play for the team, Michael's minutes got cut short. He was not used to sitting on the bench, and he got frustrated because he would be put in for a couple of minutes and just when he made a mistake whether it was a bad pass or a missed shot or turnover the coach, immediately would substitute him out of the game. I remember how much this bothered him. After the game, all I would hear is Michael expressing how all he wanted was a shot and how desperate this made him that he just quit coming and decided not to play on the team any longer. He quit instead of waiting for his chance. He had the potential, and I had seen his potential and had told him many times the qualities that he had that made him the player that he was but quit before being able to establish or acquire a position on the team. He gave up too soon. Instead of learning and finding out how he could have been a contribution to the team, he just threw in the towel too early. Many today are in that same boat, throwing in the towel too early. Instead of looking at the situation and analyzing why he was not getting enough playing time, he got anxious and decided to quit the team. As he reflects, he says that in his experience in playing basketball, he never before had been on the bench. He was always part of the starting five, but looking back he sees that God was trying to get him to sit down and observe the game, learn from the game, and now acknowledges that he quit too soon. Sometimes God will position you to sit back and look at the game, look at the story of your life. It is important you take time and contemplate where God has positioned you.

>A position is a place that is not permanent. We will always be changing positions in life. The important thing is to learn from every one of those positions about being a better person and being able to serve those God has placed around you. We as leaders have to learn how to position our youths so they can develop in the service of our churches, and teach them to go out and serve their communities so they can see the need that is around them, and awaken in them the desire to serve, and to be able to develop in our community. I am going to mention some places that you can serve in your community: shelters, food banks, habitat for humanity, state parks, city programs, hospitals,

libraries, senior citizen centers, animal shelters, and Salvation Army. These are just a few of the countless places. What you can do is first pray, and bring your request to God, and tell him to open the door. Then, step out in faith by positioning yourself to connect with the places closest to your home or church and then ask... how can we serve you? By doing this, you will not only be developing yourself but those you lead as a youth to make them servants that are strong in their faith walk by being a church who is present in demonstrating their love for God in their community.

Love this Bible text:

Pure and Genuine religion in the sight of God the Father means caring for the orphans and widows in their distress and refusing to let the world corrupt you.

Let me share with you a little story that we experienced. In 2015, it was coming around the time of thanksgiving, and we were looking for an opportunity to serve. God was preparing our hearts for something that we would never have imagined. The phrase that God gave me for that year was "Let God surprise you", and He sure did. After praying, we positioned ourselves to want to serve and began to contact nonprofits around the city of Houston. We were looking at places that were far from our church, but when we would contact these places either their numbers were out of service, no one answered, or we left voicemails. It was shocking that we were not getting a response back like all the doors were just closing on us. Until as I looked down the list of nonprofits and decided to call the last one on the list with the name Mission of Yahweh and they answered my call. We shared with them that we were looking to want to serve and do a Thanksgiving celebration with them. They were excited to hear but wanted to speak with us first. So, my friend Michael and I went to the Mission of Yahweh. When we entered the office of the director of the center, we explained our plan, and how we wanted to help and serve a Thanksgiving celebration. To our surprise, she told us some words that we never forgot, and we did not expect. The director of the Mission of Yahweh told us if we wanted to help shelter, she would direct us to other shelters and centers where we could provide a Thanksgiving celebration. We were shocked to hear this, and it was unexpected because we wanted to serve at the Mission of Yahweh, so we politely asked why? Here is why and she told us that many churches always go on holidays to do activities at the Mission of Yahweh, but that was no longer the plan. I was not going to accept a church to do activities only for holiday purposes because she had many experiences where churches would come for that particular time of the year and leave not to be seen until next year during either Thanksgiving or Christmas time. She told us that she grew up in a shelter center. By this time, our mouths dropped as her eyes began to dig deep into the past. She said it was always hurtful to me to see how the church just came during the Christmas time to make me laugh, brought me gifts, food, and have a great time, but yet I would never see them throughout the rest of the year. This left a scar within my soul for so many years I kept asking why? They never realized that in their heart to want to serve on that particular time of the year only, it left a hurt and wound in my heart because I would open my heart to them, and then never see them again. Moving forward, she told us that she wanted people who are dedicated and committed to loving and following up on the children and mothers who are homeless at the Mission of Yahweh and be able to have a consistent presence that would impact their lives.

What she shared with us really marked our lives forever. We let her know that we were going to be dedicated to being consistent and that Thanksgiving would just be the beginning. She looked at us intentionally and smiling she opened the door. Immediately we started to organize the activities, and the teams in places to make the event a reality. We got families to help with the food at church. We got the jumpers for the children, face painting for the children, photo booths for the families, and a day where they would not only remember us but where we would begin to form relationships for eternity. The day came. The place was packed. We began our program by worshipping and praising Jesus, singing songs with the children and sharing with them a message of thankfulness. Truly, we were thankful for allowing us to enter into their lives. By the end of the day, many mothers were coming to us crying and expressing how grateful they were for us coming. Truly, the ones who were grateful were us because we had seen God open a door, and not only that but it taught us a valuable lesson about serving.

From that moment, we followed up with a Christmas program where we went the next month, and there was a powerful story. I would like to share with you what happened to us. As we were leaving from the place, there was a lady that approached us from the Mission of Yahweh and gave us an envelope. I politely took it and said thank you, but she insisted that I open the envelope. As I opened the envelope, it was a Christmas card, and she said, please read it. The following words were written on that card which said: "Thank you for not looking at us as homeless people, but God's daughters." This was a moment that I would never forget. As I read those words and I looked into her eyes, I saw how she opened her heart and arms and gave me a big hug. We were left without words because we had witnessed how God was manifesting His presence in that place.

The other thing that was crazy was how God worked all this out because when it came for me to look at how far this place was from our church, I noticed that it was just down the block. Literally, it was like 5 minutes from the church. I was like what. Wait. God. Really. You are too funny. I was without words, and from that ministry was born our Outreach Youth ministry at church called Infuse Love where we have a light bulb on the front of our T-shirts, and the back it says a powerful verse that Jesus once said and continues saying to us today "Your Love for one another will prove to the world that you are my disciples." We continue going every third Sabbath of every month. We just celebrated our one-year anniversary.

The director tells us how many women have cheered up and have a sense of wanting to continue to fight. She expressed to us how the mission is not the same place it once was. The director tells us that from this relationship, there have been many more organizations that have been coming on a consistent basis and wanting to serve. There have been other churches that have joined our outreach ministry. That is exactly what we can do to impact others. That is why it is important to take advantage of the position that God has given us to do something for others and in helping other youths by positioning them in a way that they too can impact their communities. Love the story of the disciples and Jesus and how they were only twelve, and he sent them out two by two. Now many years later, we are millions. Believe this that you who are reading this book are in the position to make a change. Only you can decide when to do it.

Be a Missionary in your Backyard.

CHAPTER 14

POSITIONED TO CONQUER

When God has selected you, it doesn't matter who else has rejected you or neglected you. God's favor outweighs all opposition. You are a Winner!

Let's keep it real. No one likes to lose. We have in our innate nature to want to win. If you think about it, parents do everything possible to place their children in the position to conquer. Whether it be scholastically, spiritually, socially, athletically, parents will do whatever in their power to position their children to conquer, and reach their full potential. Just a couple weeks ago, I was watching a documentary, which by the way I love documentaries. There is something about going behind the scene and learning from different people in different places about their story. Like I said, I was on Netflix watching "At All Cost". It was looking at how young high school basketball athletes are being groomed from an early age, and how they develop these future basketball professional starts during the offseason with these Amateur Athletic Union leagues. How the AAU leagues have become industrialized and commercialized. In the documentary, it explored and looked at three different stories, but there was one story of a father and his son that intrigued me a lot. Father and son had devoted themselves to work hard for his son to be able to get a full ride scholarship to an elite basketball college program. Through their journey, the documentary depicts how many trips they have to take from coast to coast, how many basketball camps they participate in his offseason, the hard work, sweat and tears to just arrive at the goal of having a recruiter offer you a full ride scholarship. This kid would play his whole season of high school basketball, and just when many kids are entering their summer break, he was preparing to enter his AAU summer basketball league. There came the point in the documentary that his body was starting to give out. He was feeling pain and strain in his ankles leading to an injury, and just when you think it was all over, he kept fighting. It got me thinking, and at times I thought it was maybe too much. His father was maybe pushing him too hard, or maybe this was not his son's dream, but rather his father's dream. But one thing I did see was how the father had a dedication and commitment to positioning his son to conquer. Placing his son in the best position to conquer and achieve the dream. In the end, he gets a scholarship and continues his basketball career in an elite program in the country with a full ride scholarship. The point that I wanted to bring with this story is that the father positioned his son to achieve his dream. It was not easy, and it took a lot of sacrifices, but they did it. In the midst of all the opposition, rejection, and injury, they reached their objective.

      Let me share with you another experience. I just got back from getting a fresh haircut. Now the lady that cuts my hair and I have become very good friends. I mean after getting a haircut every two weeks you would think there would be a friendship built and that is exactly what has happened. As she was cutting my hair, I asked her what her New Year's resolutions for 2017 are? Being that it was January 2, 2017. She said that those were private, and as you may or may not know me I am very persistent, not nosy, so I asked her another question, "Well what's the top thing that you want to accomplish in the next couple months?" See how I switched that up. She opened up and shared with me how on January 17 she wanted to start paying her son's school so he could focus on finishing up school faster, and not worry so much about working and studying, but rather focus all his time on school. If she could start paying his tuition, he would be done in August of this year. As she is sharing this New Year's resolution, you should've seen the eyes and the smile on her face. She was determined and committed to seeing her son graduate and help him accomplish that dream of his. This mother was positioning herself and her business to be able to get him in the best position for him to finish school. She was willing to sacrifice her time, her dreams, her goals, her career, and even her life just to position her son to conquer his dream of becoming a nurse.

    It just takes me back to the Bible in Matthew 10 Jesus had recruited twelve ordinary men from all walks of life. You had a fisherman; you might have known that already, political activists and tax collectors. He called brothers, common, uncommon, rich, poor, educated and uneducated. All asked by Jesus to follow Him. To leave their jobs, professions, careers and follow him. There were two things the disciples had seen Jesus do at the beginning of his ministry. The first was his teaching, and the second one was healing. When Jesus spoke, He captivated the crowds he taught. The Bible says that no one had heard someone teach with so much authority, so much truth, so much wisdom, and so practical because He used parables which are common stories of their day to grasp the heavenly meaning. Not just that, but Jesus also was healing. Literally touching people, speaking to people or people would just touch him and bang they would be completely healed. From blind people to crippled people, to dead people to even lepers. People with all of their diseases and conditions would find complete healing in the person of Jesus. This makes me go crazy and not just that, but there was no monthly bill to that healing. He was not gathering a commission or concerned about a tip; rather he did it because the Bible says He was moved by compassion.

    Now, the disciples had witnessed all of this. Now, it was time for Jesus to position His twelve disciples to send them out. It was their turn. A good teacher not only teaches his students but positions his students to apply what they have learned. What makes a great student is not just filling himself with knowledge, but how he can use that knowledge to better others. That is exactly what Jesus was doing in Matthew chapter 10 with the twelve. Jesus calls them over the Bible says and had a team huddle with them. He then gave them the authority to cast out evil spirits and to heal every kind of disease and illness. There is a word I want us to focus on for a bit which is the authority.

    Authority, in breaking down this word, it is the ability someone greater than you permit you to do something that you did not have access to. Jesus here is handing out some power to do some very specific things. I love how clear Jesus is with his instructions to his disciples. He huddles them up (Holy Huddle) and gives them authority (power) to cast out evil spirits, heal every kind of disease and illness. Wow, Jesus hooks them up and gives them the ability and power to do some incredible things. Jesus positions them to do what the disciples up to this point had only seen Jesus do which include healing all kind of sickness and expel evil spirits. Now, here they get an opportunity not just to see it, but to be part of it. They experienced and saw with their own eyes how Jesus had done it. Jesus was saying to them now it's your turn. Jesus was positioning his disciples for a conquest. Jesus was positioning them with the power to conquer. He was setting them up for success. They had witnessed it, and now it was time to walk in it.

Now as the disciples were getting ready to head out, there were some specific instructions Jesus gave them. Have you ever been in a situation where you were about to step out from a comfortable situation? To step out into an unknown territory. To step out, and all you do is create scenarios in your head of what it is going to be like. As human beings, we do not like being in uncomfortable situations. We like to know where we are going, who we are meeting, what we are doing, and we like to know everything that we need to expect. It makes me think of our youth mission trip at our church that we conduct every year. This year, we are preparing to go to Guyana which is just a couple months away. I noticed how parents more than youths have all these questions on what to expect because their sons or daughters are going to a different country that they have never been too. Now imagine Jesus telling the parents of these youth that will be heading on this mission trip these next words:

> Don't take any money in your money belts, no gold, silver, or even copper coins. Don't carry a traveler's bag with a change of clothes and sandals or even a walking stick. Don't hesitate to accept hospitality, because those who work deserve to be fed. -Matthew 10:9-10 (NLT).

What reaction do you think you will get from the youth's parents? Or what would your mother or father do in this situation? I know my mother would be like "Son I do not think you're going on this mission trip" It sounds a little radical what Jesus was saying here, but Jesus wanted his disciples to have a complete dependence and experience where all they could rely on was His Spirit. This radical faith to know that God's got you, and He is for you. Jesus' ultimate goal is for us to receive His power and to be witnesses telling people about Him. These were the words that Jesus said later after He had resurrected from the grave and was about to ascend to heaven:

> The Father alone has the authority to set those dates and times, and they are not for you to know. But you will receive power when the Holy Spirit comes upon you. And you will be my witnesses telling people about me everywhere in Jerusalem, throughout Judea, in Samaria, and to the ends of the earth. Acts 1:7-8 (NLT)

Never forget this. You were never created to be depressed, defeated, guilty, condemned, ashamed or unworthy. You were created to be victorious. Jesus has positioned you to conquer. You are to rise and step on those things in your life that have been bringing you down. He has positioned you to speak life and to know that we are more than conquerors through Christ Jesus our Lord. Let us go. The battle is not our battle. It is the Lord's, and He will fight for us. Just position yourself for God's victory as God wipes out the enemy!

CHAPTER 15

WANT TO BE GREAT?

The life of a Christian is not about Prosperity, Power & Position but about Service, Suffering & Sacrifice Don't believe me Look at JESUS.

When you think of Greatness who do you think of? What did the person do to reach greatness? Why do you think of that person as being great?

Greatness. In 2016 the NBA finals were between the Golden State Warriors and the Cleveland Cavaliers, and it was a battle till the end. I was glued to the television. There is just something about the NBA finals. It's the culmination of a long season. During this time, many sports analysts were counting on the Warriors to take the championship because of their amazing teamwork, and also because they set the best record in NBA history 73-9. The odds were against Lebron James. Many people were saying that if he wanted to be great, he had to show up and finish games just like in the previous NBA finals he had participated in. Many people said he was not clutched down the stretch. He would not finish games in the fourth quarter. With the series 3-1 against his favor, everyone counted him out. They counted the Cavaliers losing yet another final. Therefore, they took it play by play, game by game. And by fighting their way back, they were able to tie 3-3. Now it came down to the last game. Now the question was...could Lebron James lead his team to one of the greatest comebacks in sports history? With the game on the line with 1 minute and 52 seconds, Lebron James rises to block Iguodala from the backfield. I will never forget that play. With his heart on his chest and giving it all he had, he was able to bring the first championship in 52 years to Cleveland. This is something that had never been done before.

    Greatness. Just a couple days ago Messi, made one of the most remarkable goals in soccer history capping him as the most goals scored and leading his team and an entire country of Argentina to a championship game.

    Greatness. With my friends, the question that would always rise and would be a lot of discussions was who was the best basketball player amongst us? As you can imagine, everyone had an opinion of who they thought was the best player and why. You could imagine at one point the testosterone in the room was so high that we decided to take it to the basketball court right then and there. We made a small tournament where we would see who the greatest basketball player amongst us is? These conversations would come up a lot during the intramural season in our respective Universities. Even after we had graduated, we continue to have the same conversation who is the best basketball player? Soccer player? They still continue.

Greatness brings comparisons which bring rivalries. Sports have some huge rivalries. The ones that come to mind are the Lakers vs. Celtics. Another huge rivalry that comes to mind is the Yankees vs. the Red Socks. You cannot forget soccer and its rivalries which I believe one of the biggest rivalries in soccer is Barcelona vs. Real Madrid. Think about how rivalries have begun? Whether it is between high schools, colleges, and professional sports, it all stems back to the comparisons. These comparisons have escalated to levels that through the many years not only bring out the best in players, but also there have been many fights, and tempers have flared all because of the comparison game. Think about it for one rivalry game stadiums have been burned up. Soccer fans throwing things onto the soccer pitch or throwing cups of urine on the opposing team. All because of rivalry games that began with comparisons. All in the sports arena of wanting to be great or wanting your team to be the greatest.

Think about it we always bring about comparisons of two basketball players that have retired and no longer play the game, but yet we tend to ask the question…between Kobe Bryant and Michael Jordan, who's the greatest ever to play the game? Who is the best duo? Comparisons are dangerous. I am going to take a stretch and say comparisons kill.

You might be asking then what your point is. We should just stop watching sports, stop following rivalries. Let me illustrate what I want to get to with this next story. Just a couple days ago, the American Soccer Cup was happening, and the game was between Chile & Colombia. The game was going back and forth until Chile scored two goals. Now as the teams were headed to the locker rooms for the coach's message and a strategic game plan, there was an alert that came up, and they announced that the game was going to be delayed because of the heavy storms but more because of the lightning. So the rain fell on the city of Chicago and the fans, of course, took shelter. After all was said and done, there was a team that took the field to dry up the pitch, and it hit me. The fans were getting louder and louder because they couldn't wait to see their favorite players take the pitch again, and continue the festivities, but what everyone forgot was the group of workers or volunteers who went out on the pitch and grab rain shovels and started to dry the pitch. What I noticed were these volunteers or workers might have been overlooked, and no one might remember their names, but they served the purpose of getting the soccer pitch ready for the soccer teams to get back to the game. No one will ever mention those men that squeezed the water off of that pitch. No one will think of them after the game is over. Not even the soccer players will reminisce about the effort those men did, but similar can be said to many today who work behind the scenes and have the heart for service, they won't get the spotlight and won't get the recognition. But God sees every detail of every activity we do for others, and the motives by which we are moved. He sees it, and He rewards it.

  It was the last moments on planet earth, and Jesus had just finished cleaning all the disciple's feet. They were hesitant at first, and it was truly a humbling experience to have the Son of God washing the disciple's dirty feet.

The measure of greatness in the kingdom of God differs vastly from that of the world. Our society idolizes the rich, the powerful, the beautiful, and the athletic. The world claims it is demeaning to serve others. The person who serves selflessly, lovingly, without complaint, and without seeking recognition is highly regarded in the kingdom of God.

When Jesus and His disciples entered the upper room, the disciples looked for a prominent place to sit; Jesus looked for a position to serve. As they awkwardly waited to be served, Jesus took a towel and basin and washed their feet (John 13:1-15)

We (Christians) like to refer to ourselves as servants, but we are seldom content to be treated as servants. Every day or should I say constantly, we are bombarded to adopt the world's view to be great, to focus on me, to trample the rest, and keep positioning myself for greatness. Climbing up the corporate ladder, to look for places to sit, and rule over. Yet Jesus had a contrary idea to our humanistic, selfish, egotistical lives. The King of this world was positioning Himself to serve, and most of all sacrifice His life for the salvation of this world for the chance that you and I would have the privilege to be called children of God.

The world will estimate your importance by the number of people serving you. God is more concerned with the number of people you are serving. If you struggle to be a servant, your heart may have shifted away from the heart of God. Ask Jesus to teach you selflessness, and to give you the strength to follow His example. Watch for Jesus' invitation to join Him in serving others. He will give you a heart for those around you. He will position you in places you never would imagine but ask yourself why Jesus? And remember, it is not to sit and rule, but to stand and serve. Position yourself for service. Never forget about it.

The world's system of leadership is very different from leadership in God's Kingdom. Worldly leaders are often selfish and arrogant as they claw their way to the top. (Some kings in the ancient world gave themselves the title "Benefactor," friend of the people). But among Christians, the leader is to be the one who serves best. There are different styles of leadership—some lead through public speaking, some through administering, some through relationships—but every Christian leader needs a servant's heart.

The question to ask anyone around you is this simple question: How can I serve you? Try it. See what this question unpacks, see what kind of serving opportunities come your way, but also be ready and be willing to do it. It reminds me of a story in the Bible as the disciples were arguing about who was going to be the greatest among them. Jesus had just made a public announcement that someone at that last supper table was about to betray Him, and in this conversation, it leads to who would be the greatest among them. Look at Jesus words:

> In this world, the kings and great men rule over their people, yet they are 'friends of the people'. But among you, it will be different. Those who are the greatest among you should be the lowest rank, and the leader should be a servant. Who is more important, the one who sits at the table or the one who serves?

The one who sits at the table, of course, but not here! For I am among you as one who serves. You have stayed with me in my time of trial. And just as my Father has granted me a Kingdom, I now grant you the right to eat and drink at my table in my Kingdom. And you will sit on thrones, judging the twelve tribes of Israel. (Luke 22:25-30).

We live in a world where positions have a perception of entitlement and importance. You do not have to look too far to see what many countries' governments have done to its people by their exercise of authority. The oppression and even racial discrimination to rule over people. Politicians bribe the people by painting pictures of the future, but ultimately, many are looking for an opportunity to rule or exercise their authority over the people. In yet another point that Jesus presents in his words is we are called to be different. We are not in this world to look for a prominent position to sit in, but a position to serve. Even when the people God raised to high officials in government positions like Joseph, Daniel, Esther, just to name a few, it was for the benefit of his people. God was positioning these leaders in their respective leadership positions for the salvation of His people. God will position in places to serve His people not to rule over His people. Got a little caught up, but following Jesus words, He then brings out a wide and common question that I believe is still relevant in this century, "Who is more important between the one who sits at a table or serves?" Even Jesus answers it by saying it is universally accepted that the one who sits and gets served is important, but then, he says not with my followers. Jesus was contrary to the world's idea of authority in looking to rule rather than to serve. Then Jesus presents to his friends that have stayed with him this whole time the privilege to sit on thrones when His Kingdom comes judging the twelve tribes of Israel. It is like Jesus says you all are important to me, and this world is not your home. You have been promoted in my Kingdom.

You've got a place to sit. You are going to be seated on thrones, but do not let this get to your heads. In the meantime, let us get to work and let us start to serve. Let people see something different in you. Not the hunger for the fame, acclaim, the applause, but rather for the opportunity to serve the world. My question to you is, are you seating or are you serving? Think about it…Are you just sitting around waiting for someone to serve you, to reach out to you, or are you positioning yourself for service? Whether it might be as a school teacher, mentor, coach, business professional, church leadership, etc., my question to you is to ask yourself where has God positioned you, and are you doing your best in serving His people?

CHAPTER 16

BE PATIENT WITH THE PROCESS

The Process is more important than the product

One of the hardest things is to be patient. I know I get impatient very easily for the smallest things, like waiting for my wife to get ready. I get impatient when there is traffic, and you are bumper to bumper especially in H-town (Houston) where I am currently living. Impatient when you're waiting to get on a ride at Six Flags, or the DMV waiting to get your License renewed or change the plates. Impatient when you're waiting for your friends at a restaurant who told you an hour ago that they would be there in 10 minutes. Impatient when my Hispanic people say they will be there in 5-10 minutes, and it turns out to be like 1 hour. Even with our lives, we become impatient in waiting. But let me tell you the most real statement that took me almost 15 years later to realize is this: be patient with the process. It is this statement that I keep reminding myself constantly.

Be patient with the process. There have been many moments in my life where I had planned and arranged, and God has interrupted the plans because He has got other plans. Therefore, I have come to understand that one must be patient with the process. Now I am not saying not to plan and just wing everything. What I mean is that God will at times surprise you, and you have to be willing to follow His lead. It is not easy to wait. We live in a culture today that waiting makes us impatient. Especially tell that to a person who is hungry as he is waiting in the drive-through line and then, as he orders his food, they tell him to please drive forwards to the nearest parking lot as they finalize his order.

Life is full of moments. Moments that marks your life. Through these last six months, it's been a slow process in the carrying out the vision of INCH. One of the hardest things for me, and it might be for you is to wait. I don't like waiting. Whether it's waiting for your food when you're hungry, waiting for your ride when you're already late, waiting for your wife as she is still getting dressed, can I get a witness, waiting for that shipment to arrive. No human likes to wait. We like it now and fast. We are willing to pay more for faster service and shipment because we feel like while we are waiting, we are wasting time. I don't know about you, but I am the type of person that you tell me something whether an idea, thoughts, or a problem, and I am the type of person that says "what are we waiting for? Let's do it, let's fix it". God has taught me a valuable lesson in this process. Psalms 27:14 Wait for the Lord; be strong and let your heart take courage; wait for the Lord.

Many times we want to see the product, but God wants to work in the process. We want to see the results right away. God wants to grab our attention to remind us to focus back on me. God needs to realign the visionary before he continues the vision God has intended for him to accomplish on earth. This is exactly what God has been taking me through in these last couple months.

It has not been easy because many people say I've got ADD because I cannot sit still for more than thirty seconds or else, I start getting distracted or anxious to move around or do something else. If God needs to fill and fulfill the vision He has revealed to us; we need to position ourselves to listen to His voice constantly in quiet places. In places where we shut out the noises and the gadgets that grab our attention and we take quiet time to be alone with our God.

The way I have seen God realign my life in the last couple months is by placing people on my path with the same strong desire, and passion and that see the need for it. As I was in Guyana preparing for the youth mission trip, I met many leaders in the church that feel that same desire to use sports as a platform to connect with today's generation, and eventually share with them the everlasting good news. Sports has a way of breaking down barriers and making us come together to play the game that we love. I have seen the opportunities God has opened but also gifted me with to use it for the Kingdom. For many years, I played sports which I noticed it was taking over my life. Let me explain, I could wake up at four or five in the morning to play ball, but when it came to my time with God, I was just too tired. Until I noticed as I got much older, that sport was a part of my journey, sports does not have to be my drug, but it can be the avenue or platform for me to connect with distinctive generations and break barriers for others to see Christ in us and the hope of glory. Sports can be the platform for others to see Christ in us. Sports can be the opportunity that God uses for someone to have an experience with Jesus. All of this has taken many years for me to realize. Being patient with the process is important.

Being patient takes you places. Therefore, being patient with the process is awaiting the future promise. What I mean by this is, we are all called to persevere, to keep going, to take that next step, to not give up. Our mindset should be step by step, inch by inch, and as you take those steps, it's necessary to be patient in the process. We can call it faith. Then as people of faith, we will have a culminating moment where the future promise is going to be fulfilled. There is a longing in each of our hearts as children of God to rush into the plans or figure everything out. The Creator has meant for this life to be a faith walk, a trust walk, a dependency walk. What I mean by this is you take one step at a time. The moment we begin to see life as a faith walk, a step by step, inch by inch, then we will continue to see our path light up. I know as you look back, you are not where you once were, and I guarantee you in a couple of years from now, you will not be where you are currently at. Trust me. Through this entire faith journey, do not forget to be patient, be at peace with the alignment of the assignment your heavenly daddy hands you.

Thank you for taking the time to read this book. I pray you can take with you maybe just one simple life lesson that you can apply to your life or your youth's lives. As we have walked together on this journey, our desire has been that if you are a youth to see how God wants to unlock the potential that has been placed by Him inside of you. To make you realize that there were people that have come before you, that felt incapable, felt unable, felt unprepared, but once God reminded them that He was going to be with them, step by step they were able to accomplish the assignment God had for them. You are never too young to make a great impact for God. If you are a youth leader, I pray that you unlock the youth's God-given potential that God has placed in front of you whether it is with fifty or just with one. Remember Jesus changed the world not by going big, but by going small. Jesus took twelve and changed the world with those twelve. Youth or youth leader, you do not have to look too far. You've got to look at where God has positioned you right now and begin there.

    A couple of months ago as I was coming back from the Path-finder camporee where we witnessed one hundred lives give their hearts to Jesus and be born to life through baptism. On the drive back home, one of the parents shared with me this story as we were talking about impacting and inspiring this next generation. This story just changed my life, and I want to close with it. There was a small boy who noticed on the ocean shore a vast amount of starfish. Starfish have to be in saltwater to stay alive. So, this little boy saw the starfish, and rushed down to the shore, and started to grab the starfish as fast as possible and began throwing them back into the ocean. One by one he began to throw the starfish into the ocean. There was a man who was passing by and looked at the effort of the little boy, and how he was doing everything in his power to throw as many of the starfish back into the ocean, yet he also looked at how there were thousands of starfish still lying on the ocean shore. So, the man yelled to the little boy, you are wasting your time. There are too many starfish. Surely you cannot expect to make a difference. The little boy heard the man, thought for a moment, and bent down to pick up another starfish and sent the starfish sailing back to the water. As the little boy threw the starfish, he said to the man with a smile on his face "It made a difference to that one" as he continued to bend down grab the starfish and throw them in the vast ocean.

      The little boy is you. You can also make a difference in today's world. There are many starfish that are dying and needing help. This generation is dealing with so much from abusive relationships to self-esteem issues, sex, not feeling appreciated, left out, bullied, toxic environments, drugs, gangs, party life, anger, pain and the bottom line is they need love. They need someone that truly cares about them, someone that will listen to them, someone they can trust, someone that does not look at them for who they are, but what they could become for someone to just simply believe in them. Someone who will awaken their God-given potential, show them a heavenly perspective, and position them to serve in this society. The world will be like that one man that only walks past the problem and just tries to discourage you, and try to tell you that you are wasting your time, but remember the words of that little boy as he bent down to pick up one more starfish he said "IT MADE A DIFFERENCE TO THIS ONE". Go out and make a difference today. Let us echo the words of Albert Pine that once said:

"What we do for ourselves dies with us, what we do for others and the world remains and is immortal."

INSPIRE ONE

One Life at a Time

Made in the USA
Columbia, SC
18 August 2023